SpringerWienNewYork

# ÁLVARO SIZA

VON DER LINIE ZUM RAUM

Herausgegeben von Rudolf Finsterwalder
und Wilfried Wang

FROM LINE TO SPACE

Edited by Rudolf Finsterwalder
and Wilfried Wang

SpringerWienNewYork

7	Vorwort Oliver Kruse	70	Sportzentrum Panticosa
	Preface Oliver Kruse		Sports center Panticosa
9	Von der Linie zur Figur *Wilfried Wang*	80	Museum Serralves
	From Line to Figure *Wilfried Wang*		Museum Serralves
15	Von der Linie zum Raum *Rudolf Finsterwalder*	90	Pavillon Anyang
	From Line to Space *Rudolf Finsterwalder*		Pavilion Anyang
		98	Museum Mimesis
			Museum Mimesis
		108	Wettbewerb Alhambra
			Competition Alhambra
	Projekte **Projects**	117	Biographien
			Biographies
22	Architekturmuseum Hombroich		
	Architectural museum Hombroich		
32	Raumortlabor		
	Spaceplacelab		
36	Pavillon Expo Hannover		
	Pavilion Expo Hannover		
44	Museum Iberê Camargo		
	Museum Iberê Camargo		
56	Kirche Marco de Canavezes		
	Church Marco de Canavezes		
64	Gespräch Siza — Finsterwalder		
	Conversation Siza — Finsterwalder		

Vorwort

Oliver Kruse

Preface

Nach fast 15 Jahren Planungs-, Entwicklungs- und Bauzeit hat Karl-Heinrich Müller in Verbindung mit seiner Stiftung Insel Hombroich eine Architektur von Álvaro Siza Vieira auf der Raketenstation realisiert. Ich kann mich noch gut an ein Zusammentreffen von Siza und Müller im Jahr 1995 in Hombroich erinnern. Die militärischen Gebäude der ehemaligen Nato-Raketenstation waren gerade renoviert, die Freiflächen noch unbebaut. Der vielversprechende Ort hat Siza von Beginn an interessiert. Das großzügige, ebene Terrain von dem man eine weite Aussicht genießt, verbindet sich mit der in der benachbarten Erftaue gelegenen Museumsinsel in gegensätzlicher Art. Schon in seinen ersten Skizzen ließ Siza erkennen, das sich sein Bauwerk in ortsspezifischer Weise mit der landschaftlichen Qualität der Raketenstation verbinden wird. Siza zielte auf eine Architektur, die sich sensibel in die klare Kontur der Landschaft einfügt und in diesem Sinn dem Grundsatz: »Kunst parallel zur Natur« der Insel Hombroich in architektonischer Denkart entspricht.

Ursprünglich sollte das Haus für das, auf der Raketenstation tätige Internationale Institut für Biophysik in gespiegelter Form an der Westseite der Raketenstation errichtet werden. Müller war dabei ein idealer Bauherr, der dem Architekten respektvoll planerische Freiheit einräumte und umgekehrt kompetente Ideen zur Umsetzung einbringen konnte. Sizas Projekt wurde zuerst 1996 im Rahmen der venezianischen Architekturbiennale gezeigt gemeinsam mit anderen Projekten zur Erweiterung der Raketenstation. Die Ausstellung »Hombroich Architektur« und die darin angekündigten, aus Hombroich kommenden Impulse haben einen atmosphärisch relevanten Beitrag zur damaligen Gründung der Stiftung Insel Hombroich geleistet. Dennoch sollten von Planung bis Fertigstellung des Gebäudes 15 Jahre vergehen, ein Zeichen für die Beharrlichkeit von Karl-Heinrich Müller, dessen unermüdlichem Einsatz zu verdanken ist, dass das Bauwerk auf der Raketenstation steht. Alvaro Siza ist dabei neben seiner wunderbaren Architektur für seine Geduld und seine nicht endende Unterstützung zu danken. Ebenso Rudolf Finsterwalder für die Zusammenarbeit mit Siza sowie für die Verwirklichung des Baus.

Following near 15 years of designing, planning and construction, Karl-Heinrich Müller in conjunction with his Insel Hombroich Foundation was able to realize apiece of architecture by Álvaro Siza on the site oft he former NATO missile base. I can still recall the meeting of Siza and Müller of 1995 in Hombroich. The military buildings of the former missile base had just been renovated, the landscape still vacant. From the outset, the promising location was of interest to Siza. The generous flat terrain, from which a grand panorama might be had, is connected to the neighbouring Museum Island in the valley of the Erft river in a complementary manner. Siza would already demonstrate in his first sketches that his building would connect itself in a specific local manner with the qualities of the landscape surrounding the missile base. Siza was striving for an architecture that would be placed in a very sensitive manner amongst the clear outlines of the landscape, and which would thus entirely meet the principle of "art parallel to nature" of the Museum Island Hombroich in architectural terms.

Initially Siza's building was to be constructed for the International Institute of Biophysics that was already acitve on the site of the former missile base in a symmetrically mirrored manner on the west side of the missile base. Müller was an ideal client who on the one hand provided the architect the respectful design freedom and on the other hand was able to contribute competent ideas towards the design's realization. Siza's project was first shown in 1996 in the context

Der »Siza Pavillon« ist im Jahr 2010 mit dem Einzug des Heerich Archivs, der Ausstellungsräume für Fotografie und einer Ausstellung des für die Insel so maßgeblichen Künstlers Erwin Heerich eröffnet worden. Es ist daher folgerichtig, das nun in der Folge eine Ausstellung von Werken des Architekten Alvaro Siza an erster Stelle steht. Der Siza-Pavillon setzt damit die Arbeit als Forum für räumliches Denken, als Ausstellungsraum für Arbeiten im Spannungsfeld von Architektur und Skulptur fort. Die in der Ausstellung gezeigte Gegenüberstellung von Zeichnungen und Arbeitsmodellen von Museumsbauten legt ein Hauptaugenmerk auf die intensive zeichnerische Tätigkeit. Diese nimmt einen entscheidenden Platz in Sizas Arbeitsweise und Werk ein und vermittelt in den eigenen Räumen synergetisch die Konsequenz räumlicher Vorstellungskraft.

Für die Planung und Umsetzung der Ausstellung sei den Kuratoren Rudolf Finsterwalder und Wilfried Wang an erster Stelle gedankt, die Hombroich seit vielen Jahren eng verbunden sind und in dankenswerter Weise das Konzept, Inhalte, Installation und den begleitenden Katalog erarbeitet haben. Und noch einmal möchten wir uns bei Alvaro Siza bedanken, der hiermit in eindrucksvoller Form seine Einsichten, Fragen und Arbeiten im eigenen Haus vorstellt im Lebensraum der Stiftung Insel Hombroich.

of the Architecture Biennale in Venice together with the other projects for the extension of the missile base. The exhibition "Hombroich Architecture" made a atmospherically relevant contribution to the establishment of the Hombroich Island Foundation. All the same, 15 years had to pass between design and realization, a sign of Karl-Heinrich Müller's persistence, whose indefatigable effort alone ensured that the building now stands on this missile base. Our thanks are due to Álvaro Siza for his wonderful architecture, his patience and unending support. Equally our thanks go to Rudolf Finsterwalder for his collaboration with Siza and for realizing the project.

The "Siza Pavilion" was opened in 2010 with the installation of the Erwin Heerich Archive, the exhibition spaces for photography and an exhibition of the work of the artist Erwin Heerich, who had been so influential for the Museum Island. It is therefore logical that an exhibition on the work of Álvaro Siza should follow. The Siza Pavilion thus continues with the the project of acting as a forum for spatial thinking, as an exhibition space for work between architecture and sculpture. The comparison of sketches and working models of, amongst others, museums in this exhibition emphasizes Siza's intensive sketching process. It takes on a central place in his design process and the consequences of his spatial imagination is communicated in his own building in a synergetic way.

Thanks go first and foremost to the curators Rudolf Finsterwalder and Wilfried Wang for the conception and realization of the exhibition, both of whom have been closely associated with Hombroich and who have generously developed the exhibition from the idea to the content and from the installation to the catalogue. And once more, we would like to thank Álvaro Siza for presenting in such an impressive manner his insights, questions and work in his own building, in the living context of the Museum Island Foundation.

Von der Linie zur Figur

Wilfried Wang

From Line to Figure

»Ich weiß kaum, welche Materialien ausgewählt werden sollten. Ideen kommen immateriell auf mich zu — Linien auf weißem Papier. Sobald ich sie bestimmen will, habe ich Bedenken und sie fliehen, in der Ferne wartend.«[1]

[1] Álvaro Siza, »On Materials«, in: *Álvaro Siza: Figures and Configurations: Buildings and Projects 1986–1988.* Übersetzung des Autoren, Hrsg. Wilfried Wang, Harvard University Graduate School of Design, Rizzoli, New York 1988, S. 5.

Abgesehen von anderen lang bestehenden, vermutlich dringenderen und ungelösten Fragen in Sachen des architektonischen Entwurfs, gehört es zum Schwierigsten zu wissen, wie und wann eine Linie zu Ende zu bringen ist. Die Bewertung von Sizas Werk mag mit einem Nachdenken über diese scheinbar grundlegende und einfache Frage beginnen.

Wie und wann bringt man eine Linie zu Ende? Als ein Konzept der reinen Geometrie kann eine Linie so lang und so kurz sein, wie man sie festlegen mag. Wird sie mit einem Bleistift gezeichnet, folgt sie sowohl einer synästhetischen als auch einer mechanischen Kraft. Das Konzept einer Linie existiert in ihrer wunderbaren puristischen Weise im Computer: Ihre Strichstärke ist bis auf Haaresbreite verringerbar, wobei sie gleichzeitig bis zur Unendlichkeit verlängert werden kann.

Solch abstrakter Trost wird in der Wirklichkeit zerstört. In der Wirklichkeit, wenn es um die Herstellung einer durchgängig sauberen Kante oder einer geraden Fuge geht, treten jede Menge einschränkender Umstände ein. Angefangen mit der Materialauswahl. Es gibt nicht viele Materialien, die eine derartige Beschaffenheit haben, dass sie ohne eine Art der Unterstützung ausgedehnt werden könnten, um eine Linie zu halten, und es gibt kein einziges Material,

"I scarcely know which materials to choose. Ideas come to me immaterially — lines on white paper. When I want to fix them, I have doubts and they escape, waiting in the distance."[1]

[1] Álvaro Siza, *»On Materials«*, in: *Álvaro Siza: Figures and Configurations: Buildings and Projects 1986–1988.* Ed. Wilfried Wang: Harvard University Graduate School of Design, Rizzoli, New York 1988, p.5.

Besides other lingering, probably more pressing and unresolved questions in matters of architectural design, one of the greatest difficulties is to know how and when to finish a line. We might begin our valuation of the work of Álvaro Siza with reflections on this seemingly basic and simple issue.

How and when to finish a line? As a concept in pure geometry, a line may be as long and as short as one cares to make it. Drawn with a pencil, it follows a both a synaesthetic as well as a mechanical force. The concept of a line exists in its miraculous purist form in the computer: its thickness is variable down to a hairline, while at the same time it may be extended *ad infinitum*.

Such abstract comforts are shattered in reality. In reality, when it comes to constructing a continuously neat edge or straight joint, all kinds of vicissitudes enter. Beginning with the issue of the choice of material. Not many materials

das nicht irgendwann zu Ende ist. Wählt man ein Baumaterial aus, um eine Linie »darzustellen«, muss dieses mindestens eine gleichmäßige Abmessung, Oberflächenbeschaffenheit und Farbe besitzen, um eine visuelle Kontinuität zu garantieren. Und dann bleibt immer noch die Frage, was an den beiden Enden passieren sollte. Die ersten und die letzten Elemente architektonischer Details, welche Linien darstellen, sind besonders; sie könnten unbearbeitete Schnittflächen zur Schau stellen oder sie könnten eine würdige Behandlung erfahren, die ihre Bedeutung bestätigt. In diesem Augenblick des Nachdenkens wird die Linie körperlich, sie atmet ihr eigenes Leben ein, sie verlässt die abstrakte Welt der reinen Geometrie und zeigt auf, dass schließlich eine schwierige Wahl getroffen werden musste, für die man die einsame Verantwortung trägt.

Álvaro Siza gab zu, ein Problem mit dem Beenden einer Linie zu haben, als er die Steineinfassung zum Rasen zwischen dem Büro des Dekans und dem kleinen Architekturstudio entwarf — beim Carlos Ramos Pavillon (1985–86), dem ersten Bauabschnitt der neuen Architekturfakultät in Porto. Nun, warum sollte jemand mit entwerferischen Ambitionen sich überhaupt mit Fragen des Entwurfs von Einfassungen und Landschaftsgestaltungselementen befassen, wenn effektivere Aufgaben anstehen?

Hier, in einem Raum zwischen einer alten, ehemaligen Villa, die zum Dekanat umgebaut wurde, welche dem Fluss Douro zugewandt ist, und dem auf dem Grundstück weiter hinten liegenden, zweigeschossigen Architekturstudio, sind ein Weg und ein Rasen, beide von einer Granitplatteneinfassung auf einem Betonsockel unterteilt. Die Granitplatteneinfassung ist von einer derartigen Breite, dass sie, mit entsprechender Höhe vom Boden, auch als Sitzbank genutzt werden kann. Und vor dem Eingang zum Dekanat stellte Siza eine winzige *cour d'honneur* aus den Granitplatten her; eine Art *conversation pit*, in dem eine Studentengruppe um einen Lehrer wie die Schüler um Sokrates sitzen könnte.

are capable of being stretched without requiring some form of assistance in "holding a line", and there is no material that does not end at some stage. A constructional element that is chosen to "represent" a line needs to be at least of consistent dimension, surface quality and color to ensure visual continuity. And then there is the question as to what to do with and at the two ends. The first and the last pieces of an architectural detail representing a "line" are special, they might expose the raw endings or they might be given a dignified treatment acknowledging their roles. It is at this moment of reflection that the line becomes corporeal, that it inhales a life of its own, that it departs from the abstract world of pure geometry and that finally hard choices have to be made for which one bears lonely responsibility.

Álvaro Siza admitted to the difficulty of terminating a line while designing the stone ledge along the lawn between the dean's office and the small architectural studio — the Carlos Ramos Pavilion (1985–86) — in the first phase of the new Faculty of Architecture in Porto. Now, why would anyone with architectural ambitions even bother with the design of ledges and landscape elements, when more effective tasks wait?

Here, in the space between a former mansion, converted to serve as the dean's office, facing the Douro River, and the recessive two-storey architectural studio, there is a path and a lawn separated by a granite ledge on a concrete base. The granite ledge is of such a width that, given the tight height off the ground, it can also be used as a bench. And so

Ganz am Ende dieses umrahmten Raums, welcher am anderen Ende seine Existenz als Rahmen zum Rasen weiterführt, um sich dann mit dem Architekturstudio zu vereinen, endet diese Granit-»Linie« in einem gekerbten Granitsockel, dessen Kurve sich nicht nur in einer sanften geometrischen Weise mit der wassergebundenen Decke des Fußwegs verbindet, sondern auch eine materielle Kontinuität zwischen der losen Form des Silikats, also dem Sand, und der harten Version, also dem Granit, herstellt.

Was also lediglich eine gerade Fassungslinie entlang einer Rasenfläche hätte sein können, wurde in seiner Bedeutung verstärkt. Es ist genau diese Metamorphose, die Architekten fasziniert. Wie etwas von einer Gedankenlinie zu einem erzählerischen Faden, über eine geometrische Linie zu einer Raumeinfassung und dann wieder zu einer Wiedervereinigung mit einem gewöhnlichen Boden wird, auf dem wir alle stehen können. Vom Gedanken zum Raum und zur Form — das ist die tägliche Metamorphose, die es zu begreifen gilt, die ergriffen werden muss, bevor der Gedanke eine Chance hat, vor seiner Materialisierung zu »fliehen«.

Die durch die Granitplatten geformte Sitzecke vor dem Eingang zum Dekanat ist also eine gedankliche Linie, die in einen definierten Raum umgedeutet wurde, selbst mit einem figurativen Abschluss, welcher, mit seiner gekerbten Kurve und seiner gemischten Verbundenheit mit dem Sand des Fußwegs, gleichzeitig Ende, aber auch Kontinuität ist. Man könnte so weit gehen zu behaupten, dass die Sitzecke eine Miniaturversion, eine Art Kernzelle dessen ist, was der Innenhof des Architekturpavillons auf der Ebene eines Bauwerks ist.

in front of the entrance to the dean's office, Siza decided to create a diminutive *cour d'honneur* with the granite ledge; a kind of a conversation pit that would set a group of students and a teacher in a Socratic relation.

The very end of this framed space, that at the other end leads a life of a ledge to a lawn and then merges with the architectural studio, the very end of this part of the granite "line" is formed by a scalloped granite piece whose scooped curve not only merges in a geometrically gentle way with the compacted sand of the path, but also creates a material continuity between the loose form of silica, that is sand, and the hardened version, that is granite.

So what could have just been a straight ledge bounding a lawn has been turned into something with amplified significance. It is this metamorphosis that fascinates architects. How something may turn from a line of thought, to a narrative thread, to a geometric line, to a spatial enclosure and to a reconnection with a common ground, on which we might all stand. From thought to space and form, that is the daily metamorphosis waiting to be grasped, captured before the thought has a chance to "escape" from its materialization.

The sitting area formed by the stone ledges in front of the entrance to the dean's office is thus a conceptual line turned into a defining space, even with a distinct figurative end, that, by its scooped curve and its compound affinity to the path's sand, is termination and continuity at the same time.

One might even go as far as claiming that the sitting area is the miniature, nucleic version of what the courtyard of the architectural pavilion is at the scale of a building.

Während wir also unsere »reine Bauwerksbrille« tragen, stumpfen unsere Sinne für jene Verbindungen ab, die auf einer viel grundlegenderen Basis stattfinden; Verbindungen, die in der Lage sind, sich zu größeren, dreidimensionalen Wesen, architektonischen Körpern zu ändern, und all diese hatten den Anfang ihres wirklichen Lebens im dünnen Strich einer gezeichneten Linie auf weißem Papier.

In der simplen Welt des kalten Rationalismus ist Faulheit der Bruder der Konsistenz. Zu groß ist die Versuchung, eine Linie unentwegt, unverändert, unbeendet zu lassen. Der universelle Raum, in dem eine geometrische Matrix rücksichtslos auf leider eben unregelmäßige Topographien aufgetragen wird, ist die andere Seite der von Menschen erschaffenen Faulheit. Es ist lediglich der Klang, der das Konzept des »universellen Raums« umgibt, welcher einen intellektuellen Nimbus besitzt.

In Sizas frühen Projekten sehen wir Gedankenfäden zu architektonischen Kontinuitäten werden. Nehmen wir beispielsweise den Grundriss der Schwimmbadanlage in Leça de Palmeira (Matosinhos, 1961–66). Hier, auf dem Papier, sind Linien in die Küstentopographie eingeschrieben: Felsen, Sand und die Küstenstraße. Wären diese Linien nicht dem Kopf einer Person entsprungen, die in der Lage ist, sich die Wirklichkeit vorzustellen, würden diese Linien lediglich graphische Gesten bleiben. All diejenigen, die diese Plattformen besuchen und benutzen, die die Zwischenräume bewohnen und im Pool schwimmen, würden ihrerseits nicht unbedingt die Schritte verstehen, die notwendig sind, um diese architektonischen Ordnungsmittel zu einer sublimen Wirklichkeit werden zu lassen. Die Wirklichkeit wird verkannt. Und trotzdem ist der Gedankensprung von der graphischen Syntax, die in der Zusammenstellung der Linien vorhanden ist, und in der weder eine menschliche Aktivität noch Licht oder Schatten seine Heimat gefunden hat, zu

And so, while we wear our "building-only-spectacles", we become oblivious to the grander connections that are made at a much more basic scale; connections that are capable of metamorphosizing into larger, three dimensional beings, bodies of architecture, and all of which begin their real life in the thin thread of a drawn line on white paper.

In the simplistic world of cool rationalism, laziness is the brother of consistency. Too great the temptation to let a line continue unabated, untransformed, unending. Universal space, where a geometric matrix is ruthlessly superimposed on inconvenient topographies, that is the other side of man-made sloth. Only the notion of "universal space" has an intellectually elevated ring to it.

In Siza's earlier projects we see threads of thought turn into architectural continuities. Take the plan of Leça de Palmeira Swimming Pool. Here, on paper, lines are inscribed into the coastal topography: rocks, sand and the marginal avenue. Were these lines not coming from the mind of a person capable of imagining reality, these lines would remain as mere graphic gestures. Anyone who has visited and used the platforms, inhabited the walled spaces, swum in the pool, would not necessarily understand the steps needed to transform these architectural ordering devices into a sublime reality. One takes the reality for granted. And yet the imaginative leap between the graphic syntax contained in the continuous assembly of lines, in which neither human activity nor light or shade has as yet found its home, to the

Von der Linie zur Figur

den verschiedenen Dimensionen der Gebäudehülle, zur Zeit und zum Raum, von enormer Größe. Die Streifen von Wänden, Rampen und Plattformen sind kein formalistisches Spiel, sondern, sie verknüpfen alltägliche Erfahrungen mit der allmählichen Wertschätzung der intelligenten wie auch poetischen Anwendung von Materialien.

Im Rocha Ribeiro Haus (Porto, 1960–62) und später im Manuel Magalhaes Haus (Porto, 1967–70) meistert Siza das Zusammenspiel von Flächen und Volumen in der Art, dass subtile Kreisbewegungen sowohl im Grundriss als auch im Detail beobachtet werden können (zum Beispiel hat das Rocha Ribeiro Haus regelmäßig abgesetzte Wände, die kreisförmig angeordnet sind, ein Muster, welches auch in der Detaillierung der Fensterrahmen und deren Läden erkennbar ist).

Von der Banco Pinto & Sotto Mayor (Oliveira de Azeméis, 1971–74) zum Museum Iberê Camargo (Porto Alegre, 1998–2008) besteht eine klare Linie des Denkens und ein steter Prozess der Entwurfsforschung. Obwohl sich die beiden Bauten in grundverschiedenen Situationen befinden, bezieht Siza die möglichen begrenzenden Flächen und Koordinaten aus der Umgebung, sei diese nun ein städtebaulicher Kontext oder ein ehemaliger Steinbruch. Die scheinbar unausweichliche Logik der Nutzungsverteilung (also in den beiden Fällen der Bank und des Museums eine Verdichtung der Kernfunktionen im rückwärtigen Bereich und die Anordnung der formaleren Räume mit ihrer Möglichkeit der skulpturalen Behandlung vorne) befreit den Entwurf zu einer letztlich delikaten Balance zwischen überraschenden Kompositionen und, wie sich im Laufe der Analyse feststellen ließe, einer nachvollziehbaren formalen Logik. In den beiden Fällen der Banco Pinto & Sotto Mayor und des Museums Iberê Camargo sind die Hauptfassaden durch belebte Linien und ungewöhnliche Kurven dominiert. Die tektonischen Elemente der Bankfassade beziehen sich auf Kernmaße

different dimensions of enclosure, time and space, is an enormous one. The striations of walls, ramps and platforms are no formalist games, but create a conjunction of quotidian experience and gradual appreciation of the intelligent as well as poetic application of materials.

In the Rocha Ribeiro House (Porto, 1960–62) and later in the Manuel Magalhaes House (Porto, 1967–70), Siza masters the interplay of planes and volumes such that subtle rotational movements can be noticed in plan and detail (for example, the Rocha Ribeiro House has consistently offset walls following a rotational order, a pattern hinted at in the detailing of the window frames and their shutters).

From the Banco Pinto & Sotto Mayor (Oliveira de Azeméis, 1971–74) to the Fundação Iberê Camargo (Porto Alegre, 1998–2008) there is clear line of thinking and a constant process of research. Though located on distinct sites, Siza draws potential delimiting planes and coordinates from the context, be it an urban construct or an abandoned stone quarry. From this, the seemingly inescapable logic of the disposition of the program (in both cases of the bank and the museum a compaction of the hard program to the "rear" and the honorific spaces open to more sculptural a treatment to the front) liberates the design to what ultimately is a delicate balance between surprising compositions and, in the course of analysis, a traceable formal logic. In both the Banco Pinto & Sotto Mayor and the Fundação Iberê Camargo, the configurations' public face is dominated by animating lines and unusual curves. The Banco's façade armatures relate to significant dimensions of the neighboring buildings.

der benachbarten Bauten. Im Falle des Museums Iberê Camargo spielt Siza die eher stumme, gekurvte Hauptwand der Straßenseite gegen drei freischwebende Rampenhüllen aus: eine Hommage an Lina Bo Bardis SESC Fábrica da Pompeia (São Paulo, 1977–86) sowie ein Anklang an Sizas eigenen Innenraum der Banco Borges & Irmão (Vila do Conde, 1978–86). In Bezug auf die Welt der Ideen ist eine Linie ein Gedankenfaden. Eine Linie auf der Ebene der Architektur ist ein Kompositionsmotiv, welches im ganzen Gebäude anzutreffen ist. In Bezug auf ein architektonisches Lebenswerk wird die Linie durch die unterschiedlichen Arten der Beständigkeit, die von dem einen zum anderen Bau besteht, erkannt. Allerdings sollte keine dieser Linien als in sich wertvoll erachtet werden. Es mag vielleicht für Kalligraphen zutreffen, dass Kontrolle und Ausführung, Ausdruck und Stil ihrer Schriften qualitative Kategorien sind. Für Architekten fand die Ära der flotten Darstellung, der theoretischen Stimmigkeit, eines unveränderten Stils mit dem Ausbruch des 2. Weltkriegs ihr Ende. Der Verrat an den gesellschaftlichen und kulturellen Idealen der Moderne wurde mit der mechanistischen Produktion der Massenvernichtung beendet, diese selbst eine logische Folge des Aspekts des Modernismus, in die sich der ökonomischer Rationalismus eingekauft hatte. Heute mag Sizas Arbeit von vielen als vorbildlich erachtet werden, dennoch sind die Bedingungen ihrer Verwirklichung, die geduldige und intensive Suche nach der richtigen Figur als Ergebnis der Umzeichnung unendlich vieler Möglichkeiten, weiter von der täglichen Wirklichkeit entfernt, als die Verfechter von Sizas Beispielhaftigkeit zugeben würden.

    Das heißt dennoch: Lasst uns wieder Linien auf Papier zeichnen. Nur durch das Zeichnen von Linien auf Papier kann die Architektur wieder jene Figuren erfassen, die immer schon zu entfliehen drohten.

In the case of the Fundação Iberê Camargo, Siza plays off the mute curvaceous principal wall against the three exposed ducted ramps: homage to Lina Bor Bardi's SESC Fábrica da Pompeia (São Paulo, 1977–86) and reminiscence of Siza's own interior of the Banco Borges & Irmão (Vila do Conde, 1978–86).

    A line in conceptual terms is a thread of thought. A line at the level of a piece of architecture is a compositional device that may be traced throughout a building. A line in terms of a life's work in architecture is established by the different forms of continuities that can be identified from building to building. But, none of these lines should be mistaken to be valuable per se. While it is true that for calligraphers the control and execution, expression and style of their writings are qualitative categories, for architects the era of the dashing presentation, of theoretical consistency, of an immutable style, came to an end with the outbreak of World War 2. The betrayal of the social and cultural ideals of modernism came to an end in the mechanical production of mass destruction, itself a logical conclusion of that side of modernism into which economic rationalism had bought. Today, the work of Álvaro Siza may be regarded by many as exemplary, though the conditions of its production, the patient and intense search for the right figure out of the delineation of innumerable possibilities laid out in sketches, is further from the daily reality than most proponents of the exemplary nature of Siza's position would care to admit.

    Nevertheless, in summary: let's draw lines on paper again. Only by drawing lines on paper will architecture recapture those figures that are always in danger of wanting to escape.

Von der Linie zum Raum
Analyse eines Entwurfsprozesses

Rudolf Finsterwalder

From Line to Space
Analysis of a design process

Álvaro Sizas Architektur nimmt eine Sonderstellung in der Architekturgeschichte der Moderne ein, sowohl die plastische, skulpturale Qualität als auch die Kontrolle von Raum und Licht lassen uns immer wieder staunen. Räumliche Szenarien, sowohl im Außen- als auch im Innenraum, von außergewöhnlicher Spannung und Atmosphäre entstehen an den verschiedensten Bauplätzen rund um den Globus. Ineinander fließende Räume, die auch ihre Umgebung einbeziehen, schaffen eine eigene Welt, einen eigenen Kosmos, die Welt des portugiesischen Kosmopoliten Álvaro Siza.

Implantação Am Anfang jedes Entwurfs steht eine Analyse des Ortes, das Finden der richtigen räumlichen Ordnung des gesamten Ensembles, der bestehenden Bauten, der Landschaft und seiner Architektur. Das Wichtigste ist die »implantação«, ein unübersetzbarer Terminus, der das Einfügen der Architektur in ihre Umgebung bezeichnet. Nach einer intensiven Analyse der Situation wird der Baukörper in seine Umgebung »implantiert«, dabei spielen alle erdenklichen Parameter eine Rolle. Die Topografie, die Orientierung zur Sonne, die Erschließung, das Programm des Gebäudes, Höhenbezüge und Fluchten und vieles mehr werden verinnerlicht und münden in einen ersten Entwurf. Die einzelnen Komponenten werden nicht additiv gedacht, sondern integral und organisch.

Gelegentlich werden Detail-Themen herausgehoben, die in diesem speziellen Fall besonders wichtig erscheinen, das kann z.B. auch ein haustechnisches oder ein konstruktives Thema sein.

The architecture of Álvaro Siza has an exceptional position in history of modern architecture. Along with the sculptural quality, the control of space and light amazes us again and again. Spatial scenarios with extraordinary tension and atmosphere, both on the interior and exterior, are rising at different sites all over the world. Spaces that flow into each other, while also integrating their environment, create a special world, a special cosmos, the world of the Portuguese cosmopolitan Álvaro Siza.

Implantação At the beginning of every project there is an analysis of the site, a search of the right spatial organization of the whole ensemble, the existing buildings, the landscape, and his architecture. The most important is the "implantação", a term difficult to translate that signifies the inserting of the building in its environment. After an intense analysis of the situation, the volume is implanted in its site; therefore a lot of parameters are incorporated. The topography, orientation to the sun, access, the building program, relationship of heights and alignments and a lot more are internalized and lead to a first draft. The single components are not an additional after-thought but integral and organic. Sometimes details are emphasized, which are considered fundamental; that could be based on a technical or construction theme.

Sketches Siza develops the form of the buildings from the very beginning using three-dimensional sketches. He is a master with the pencil, developing his own significant style. For Siza, thinking and sketching are one in the same. The first sketches are tested with simple small scale models and studied. There are no renderings; the architecture is

Skizzen Die Form der Gebäude wird von Anfang an hauptsächlich über dreidimensionale Skizzen entwickelt, Siza ist ein meisterhafter Zeichner, der über die Jahre seinen eigenen markanten Strich entwickelt hat. Gedacht wird mit dem Stift, für ihn ein Muss. Die ersten Entwürfe werden mit einfachen kleinmaßstäblichen Modellen überprüft und weiterentwickelt. Renderings gibt es nicht, die Architektur wird mit dem Stift und dem Modell entwickelt, was seine Architektur auch wesentlich prägt. Es wird um die Ecke gedacht, nicht nur zweidimensional mit den Rissen. Jede Ecke wird kontrolliert, jede Seite des Gebäudes wird entwickelt und gestaltet, es gibt keine »vergessenen« Seiten, kein »Try and Error«-Prinzip, wie es das Arbeiten mit dem Rechner evoziert. Die Architektur entsteht durch das Denken, nicht durch Zufälle. Seine für ihn typischen schwarzen Skizzenhefte begleiten ihn auf jeder Reise und in ihnen wird ständig an den verschiedenen Projekten weitergedacht und gearbeitet. Auch die Arbeit an den verschiedenen Projekten erfolgt organisch, es gibt Beziehungen und wechselseitige Einflüsse.

Modelle Dieses Prinzip des Entwerfens mit den Skizzen und dem Modell wird über alle Planungsphasen durchgehalten, die zweidimensionalen Pläne sind überwiegend für die Umsetzung auf der Baustelle, nicht für den Entwurfsprozess. Manche Dinge werden auch vor Ort entschieden, direkt im 1:1 Modell der Situation. So sind z.B. die Mauern der Schwimmbecken in Leca de Palmeira von Siza auf der Baustelle festgelegt worden, was einen wesentlich sensibleren Umgang mit dem Bestand, den Felsen und dem Meeresspiegel ermöglicht.

Mit dieser seiner Methode gelingt es Siza, hochkomplexe Räume zu kontrollieren oder eher zu komponieren. Ein Höhepunkt dieser Modellbaukunst war vielleicht das Modell zu seinem Museum »Mimesis« in Korea, das Modell war in einem begehbaren Maßstab gebaut, um wirklich vor allem die Decke und den Einfall des Sonnenlichts überprüfen und kontrollieren zu können.

evolved by pencil and model, which is engraved in his architecture. He is constantly thinking of every aspect of the building not just two-dimensional with the technical drawings. Every corner is controlled, every side of the building is evolved and designed, there are no forgotten sides; no try and error principal like working with the computer. Thinking develops the architecture, not by chance. His typical black books accompany him on every journey and in them he is constantly thinking and working on different projects. Even the work on various projects is evolved organically, through mutual relationship and influences.

Models This principle of designing with sketches and models is maintained over all phases of planning. The two-dimensional technical drawings are mainly for the realization on the site, not for the form finding process. Some items are even decided on the site, directly in the 1:1 model of the situation. For example, the walls of the pools in Leca de Palmeira were defined by Siza on the site, which allows a much more sensitive relationship with the location, the rocks and the sea level. With this personal method, he is better able to compose and control highly complex spaces. An example of the art of model building was the model for the "Mimesis" museum in Korea. This model was built at a scale to walk through, to be able to control and to test the ceiling and to study the degree of the sunlight.

Organische Architektur Álvaro Siza folgt einer sehr organischen Denkweise, ähnlich der Frank Lloyd Wrights, der auch versuchte, alle für die Architektur relevanten Themen in ein Gebäude und seine Außenanlagen zu fassen. So ist es auch bei Siza, kein noch so kleines Ding wird übersehen, die Haustechnik, die Beschilderung, alles wird von ihm gedacht und gestaltet. Diese Konsequenz in der Umsetzung ist sehr außergewöhnlich und macht den Reiz seiner Architektur aus. Es entstehen Räume mit einer sehr starken Atmosphäre, die zwar immer seine Handschrift trägt, jedoch auch immer mit dem Ort harmoniert. So ist z.B. das Architekturmuseum Hombroich ein Bau, der ein Material aus der Gegend, den dunkel gebrannten Klinker, aufnimmt, ihn aber im Detail anders als gewohnt einsetzt, es werden z.B. keine sichtbaren Stürze geplant, sondern der Klinker fließt wie eine Haut über das Volumen, was die plastische Wirkung steigert. Mit der niedrigen Gebäudehöhe reagiert Siza auf die weite, flache Landschaft der Gegend, verzahnt den Bau mit der Landschaft und schafft eine Referenz auf die Backsteinbauten Mies van der Rohes, von dem sich einige Häuser in der weiteren Umgebung finden.

Raumplan Wenn man sich der Raketenstation nähert, kann man nur die Dachkante des Baus erkennen, verliert das Gebäude beim Parken ganz aus den Augen; erst wenn man durch die bestehenden Erdwälle hindurchkommt, sieht man es, d.h. eine lange Wand, die einem den Ausblick verstellt, man muss sich zuerst drehen, um den weißen, vorgestellten Eingang zu erkennen, der den Besucher ins Gebäude führt. Auch im Inneren muss man sich um zwei Ecken bewegen, ehe man in den zentralen Raum gelangt und den Ausblick in den Hof der u-förmigen Anlage genießen kann. Erst hier im Hauptraum des Museums kann man das Volumen lesen und den Baukörper verstehen, nichts wird einem sofort präsentiert, sondern man muss sich den Bau nach und nach erschließen, ein durchaus erotischer Prozess.

Organic Architecture Álvaro Siza's way of thinking is very organic, similar to Frank Lloyd Wright, who also tried to integrate all relevant items in a building and surrounding. So it is with Siza, not even the little thing is overlooked, the building equipment, signage, all of it thought and designed by him. This consistency in realization is exceptional and makes the difference in his work. Rooms with a strong atmosphere are created, they always show his signature, but also harmonize with their environment. For example, the Architectural Museum Hombroich is a building built with material of this area, the dark-fired brick, but he uses it in a different way. There are no visible lintels, but the brick is flowing like a skin over the volume, what enhances the sculptural effect. With the low height of the building Siza is reacting to the flat landscape of the site, connecting the house with the surrounding and creating a reference to the brick buildings by Mies van der Rohe, which are located nearby.

"Raumplan" When one is coming closer to the Missile Station there is only the roof of the building visible, while parking it is completely out of sight. Only when one comes through the existing earth mounds can the building be seen; in front of a long wall, blocking the view, one has to turn around to recognize the white entrance, which leads the visitor into the museum. Even in the inside one has to turn around two corners before reaching the main room and can enjoy

Anhand der im Katalog gezeigten Skizzen kann man gut ablesen, wie Siza das Gebäude wie eine riesige Plastik entwirft; beispielsweise den Baukörper selbst, der sich nach außen mit der Umgebung verzahnt und so wiederum als Skulptur interessanter wird. Simultan wird ein funktionierender Innenraum entwickelt, der sowohl Beziehungen zum Außenraum herstellt als auch Innenräume mit eigener Qualität schafft.

Denken und Wachsen   Den meisten Architekturen ist es anzusehen, wie viel Zeit in ihren Entwurf investiert wurde. Bei Álvaro Siza ist es auffällig, wie seine Projekte an den verschiedenen Problemen in der Entwurfsphase wachsen. Jedes Lösen einer neuen Herausforderung, eines neu aufgetauchten Problems macht das Gebäude interessanter, lässt es mehr mit der Umgebung verwachsen. Die Probleme fordern ihn heraus, den Entwurf zu überarbeiten, durchzudenken und zu verändern. Im Falle des Architekturmuseums Hombroich etwa tauschte der Bauherr den Bauplatz, wollte aber den Entwurf beibehalten, was zu einer intensiven Auseinandersetzung mit dem neuen Ort und der »implantação« des Baus führte. Den ca. 65 m langen Baukörper in ein unebenes Gelände einzufügen war eine Herausforderung, macht aber heute den besonderen Reiz der Architektur aus. Den Bauten Sizas ist anzusehen, wie sie an den Herausforderungen gewachsen sind, wie gut sie durchgearbeitet und entwickelt sind.

the view to the U-shaped courtyard. Only here in the central room of the museum can one understand the volume and the project, nothing is presented at once, but has to be revealed step by step, a quite erotic process. With the help of the sketches shown it's possible to understand, quite well, how Siza develops a building like a huge sculpture. For example, the volume itself is interlocked with the landscape and so becomes more interesting as a sculpture, simultaneously a functional interior space is designed. This relationship between outer space and inner space creates their own unique quality.

Thinking and Growing   In most architecture it is visible how much time has been invested in the design. In Álvaro Siza's case, its obvious how his projects grow with the various problems that are encountered during the planning process. Every solution to a new challenge or problem makes the building more interesting; engaging more with its surrounding. The problems challenge him to revise the project, to think about it and to change it. In the case of the Architectural Museum Hombroich, the client changed the site, but wanted to keep the project, which lead to an intense debate over the new site and the "Implantação" of the building. To implant a 65 m long building in a complicated topography was a challenge, but now it is integral to the appeal of the building. One can see at Siza's buildings, how they met each challenge, and how well they are worked through and developed.

Detail   Alles in den Architekturen Sizas ist entworfen, es gibt keine vergessenen Ecken. Da seine Bauten auf das wesentliche reduziert sind, kann man die Vielzahl von Details wahrnehmen. Alle Teile der Bauten stehen in Beziehung zueinander, das Kleine wird aus dem Großen entwickelt und wird in ihm wieder reflektiert. Um die Kontrolle nicht zu verlieren, gibt es vor allem gedachte vertikale Raster, die meist aus den Steigungen der Treppen generiert werden, so dass Höhenbezüge entstehen, die auch in den komplexesten Räumen ein Ineinanderfließen der Linien garantieren, keine Höhe wird willkürlich festgelegt, alles steht in einer Beziehung zueinander, ist organisch gedacht.

Dieses Entwickeln von Architektur aus den bestehenden Verhältnissen heraus lässt jedesmal einen neuen »Siza« entstehen, der seine Handschrift trägt, aber auch von seiner Umgebung geprägt wird. So entstehen immer neue Architekturen, die einen überraschen und erstaunen. Siza kopiert nicht seine eigenen Bauten, sondern er erfindet immer wieder neue Dinge, was in zu einer Ausnahmeerscheinung seiner Generation macht.

Details   Everything in Siza's architecture is designed; there are no forgotten corners. Because his buildings are reduced to the essentials, one can realize the quantity of details. All parts of the buildings relate to each other; the small is developed out of the big and reflected in the small again. To not loose control, there is an imaginary vertical grid, mostly generated by the steps of the stairs, so a height relation is created, that guarantees a continuity of lines even in the most complex buildings. No height is deemed insignificant; everything is related to each other, is thought of organically.

This development of architecture out of the existing situation always creates a new "Siza", bearing his signature, but is also influenced by his surrounding. All the time a new architecture is created, that surprises and astonishes. Siza never copies his own buildings, but always creates new things; this makes him special among his generation.

Projekte Projects

◂ *Siza im Modell zum Mimesis Museum / Siza in the Mimesis museum model*

Siza Pavillon

Museum für plastisches Gestalten und Architektur,
Insel Hombroich, Deutschland (1995–2008) **Mit Rudolf Finsterwalder**

Siza Pavilion

Museum for Sculpture and Architecture,
Hombroich, Germany (1995–2008) **With Rudolf Finsterwalder**

Poetisch ist der Naturbegriff von Álvaro Siza und so ist auch sein Projekt, das Kulturinstitut, in die Landschaft eingefügt. Kommt man auf der Raketenstation der Insel Hombroich an, so ist zuerst nur das Dach des Gebäudes sichtbar. Über eine inszenierte Wegführung gelangt der Besucher zwischen den Wällen hindurch zum Eingang. Betritt er das Gebäude, so erreicht er nach einer Drehung den Hauptraum, der ihm über einen spektakulären Ausblick die Intention des Gebäudes erschließt. Alle Räume orientieren sich um einen Innenhof, der einen gefassten Blick in die Landschaft und auf Düsseldorfs Skyline bietet. Raumgreifend öffnet sich das Kulturinstitut zur Landschaft, akzentuiert die vorhandene Topografie. An einem Ausleger des Baus hängt ein Anbau, das Photoarchiv, das dem Volumen des Entwurfes zusätzlich Spannung verleiht.   Die Außenwände sind mit dem gleichen unregelmäßigen Klinker aus Abbruchhäusern verkleidet wie die bestehenden Gebäude der Insel. Massive Eichenholzbalken bilden Tragwerk und sichtbare Decke des eingeschossigen Baus zugleich. Ein wenig ist der Fußboden innen über dem umgebenden Erdreich erhaben, ohne den Kontakt zur Landschaft zu verlieren. Der flach gehaltene Bau betont mit seinen niedrigen Fenstern und nicht hohen Räumen dieses horizontale, landschaftliche Motiv. Der Boden ist wie die Decke aus Eichenholz, die Wände sind weiß. Für die Bekleidung der Bäder wird der gleiche, fast weiße portugiesische Kalkstein verwendet wie für die Fensterbänke und den vorgestellten Eingang.   Genutzt werden soll der Bau als Architekturmuseum, das die Sammlung von architektonischen Modellen, Zeichnungen usw. der Stiftung Insel Hombroich zeigt. So sollen alle Architekten, die für die Stiftung geplant haben, vertreten sein. Im Fotoarchiv, das von Volker Kahmen geleitet wird, wird eine bedeutende fotografische Sammlung archiviert.

Álvaro Siza's conception of nature is poetic and such is the placement of the Cultural Institute into the landscape. Arriving at the Raketenstation of Hombroich Museum Island, the visitor at first can only catch a glimpse of the building's roof. A carefully staged path leads the visitor through earthen walls to the main entrance. Entering the museum, the main space is reached after a turn, revealing with the help of a spectacular view the main intention of the building. All rooms are orientated around a central court, offering a framed view of the landscape and the distant skyline of Düsseldorf. Embracing the space, the cultural institute opens itself to the landscape, accentuating the existing topography. The photographic collection is housed in a wing of the building, providing additional tension to the overall composition.   The exterior walls are clad in the same variegated brick as the existing Erwin Heerich buildings of the Foundation. The bricks were recovered from old houses. Solid oak beams support the roof and at the same time they form the visible ceiling of the single-story building. The ground floor is raised a little above the surrounding agricultural fields so as not to lose the contact with the environment. With its low windows and not very tall rooms the low volume accentuates the horizontal dimension and its relation to the landscape. The floor is of oak boards, the walls are painted white. The almost white Portuguese lime stone is used for the restrooms, the entrance porch and the window sills.   The building is intended to be used as a gallery to exhibit the sculptural and architectural collection of the Foundation. All architects building for the Foundation would be exhibited here. The photographic archive, curated by Volker Kahmen, is considered to be one of the most important collections of photography.

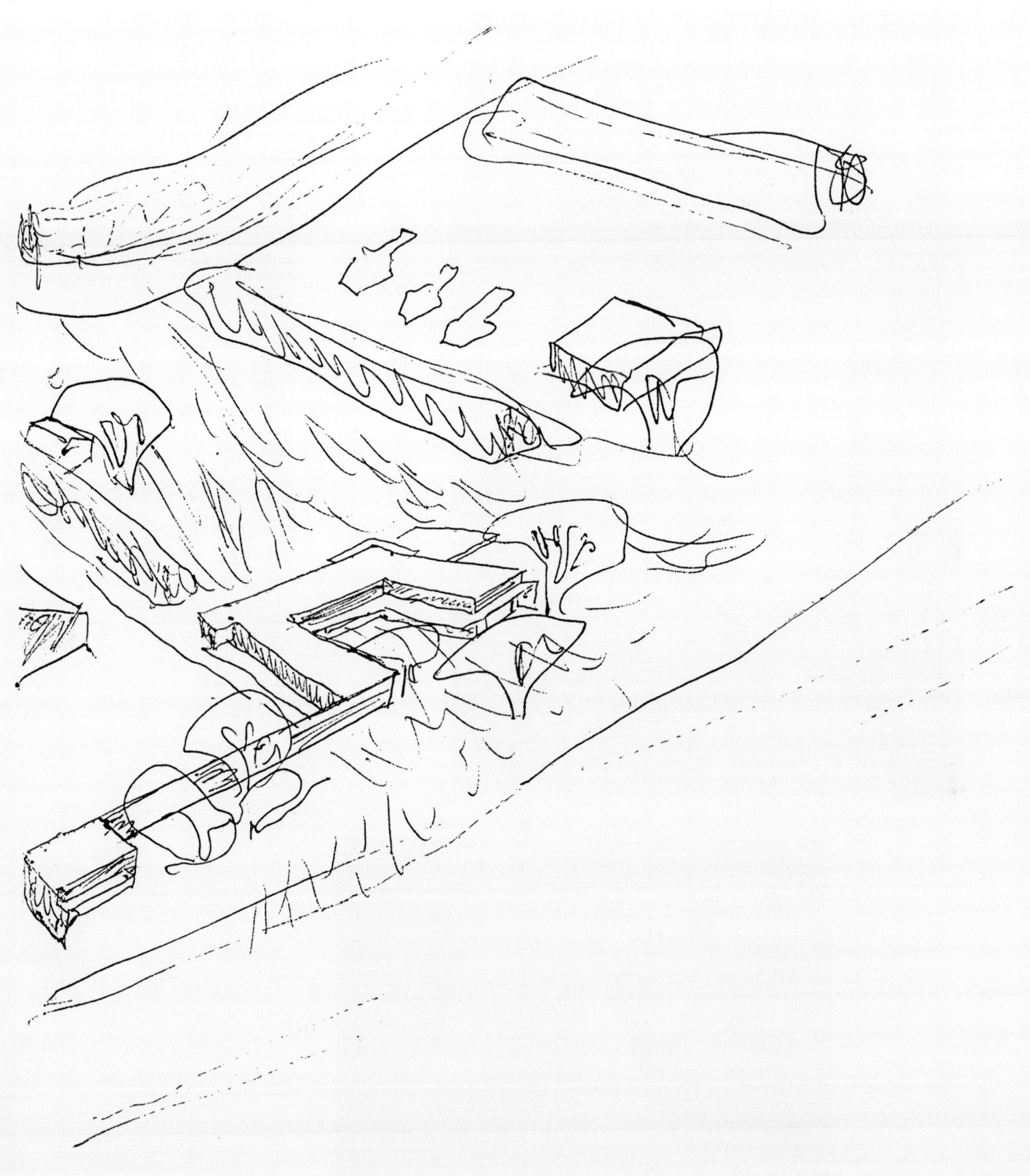

Rampe zum Anbau / Ramp to Annex

Blick vom Foto-Archiv / View from Photo Archive

1	Haupteingang	11	Fotoarchiv Eingang
2	Foyer	12	WC
3	Sekretariat	13	Technischer Bereich
4	Ausstellung	14	Fotoarchiv
5	WC (Damen)		
6	Küche		
7	WC (Herren)		
8	Technischer Bereich		
9	Auditorium		
10	Archiv Heerich		

1	Main Entrance	11	Photo Archive Entrance
2	Foyer	12	WC
3	Secretary Office	13	Technical Area
4	Exhibition Room	14	Photo Archive
5	WC (Ladies)		
6	Kitchen		
7	WC (Gentlemen)		
8	Technical Area		
9	Auditorium		
10	"Heerich" Archive		

Modell 1. Bauplatz / Model former site

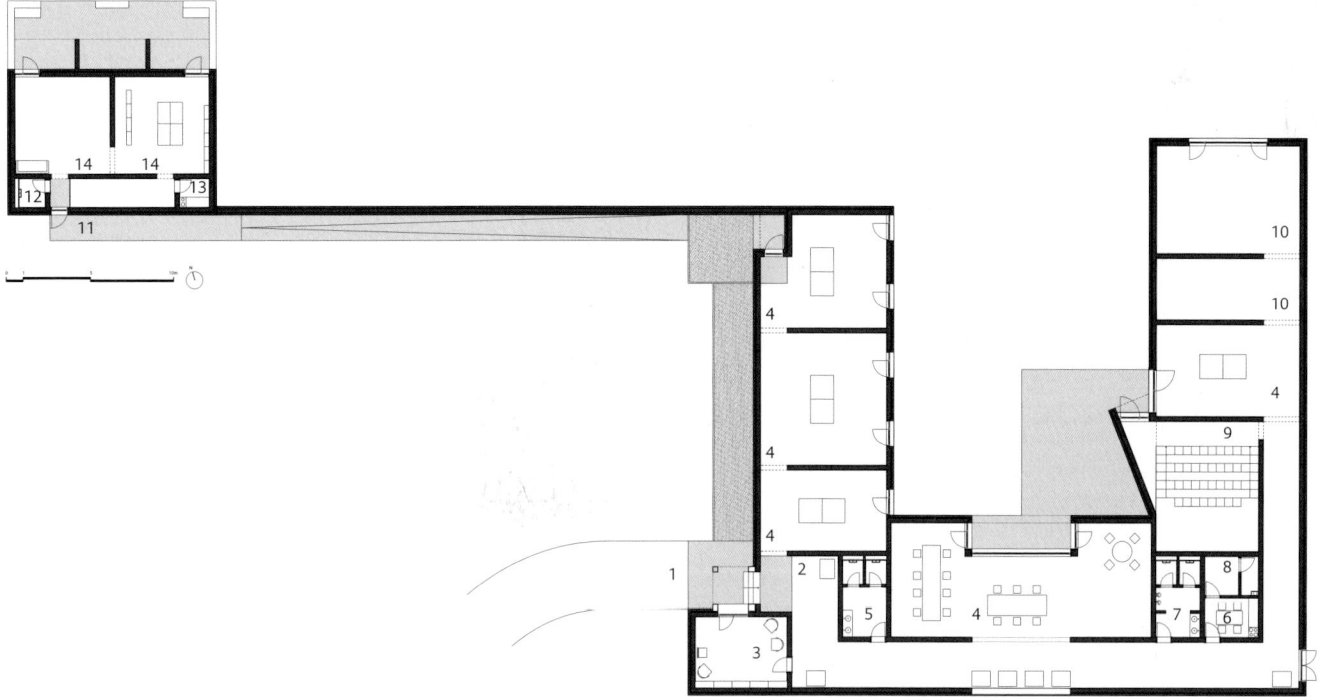

Grundriss Erdgeschoss / Ground floor plan

Architectural museum Hombroich

Terrasse Foto-Archiv / Photo Archive terrace

Skizze Eingang / Entrance sketch

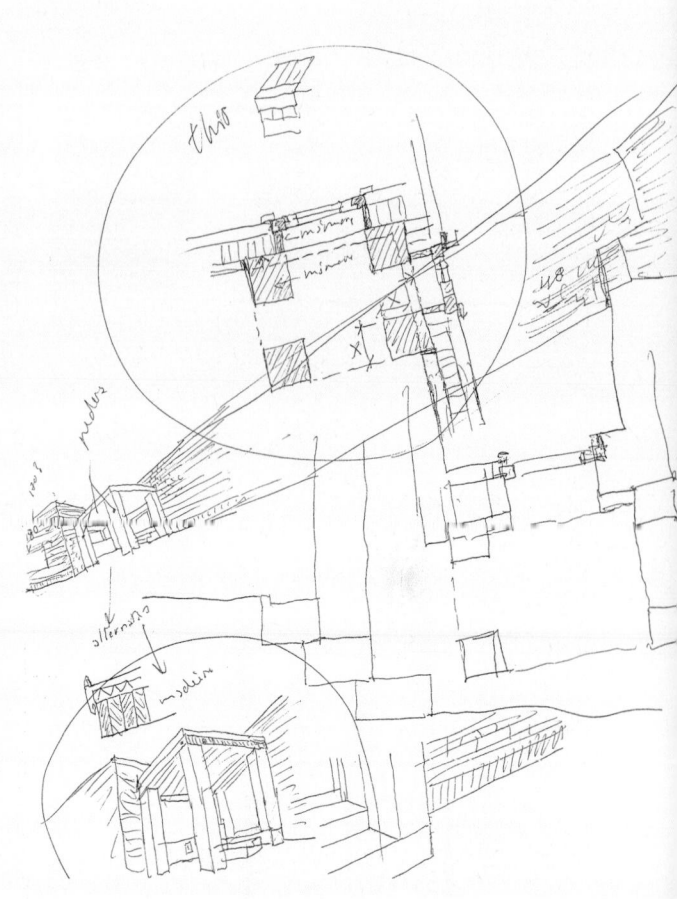

Haupteingang / Main entrance

26 Architekturmuseum Hombroich

Umgebungsmodell alter Bauplatz / Site model former site

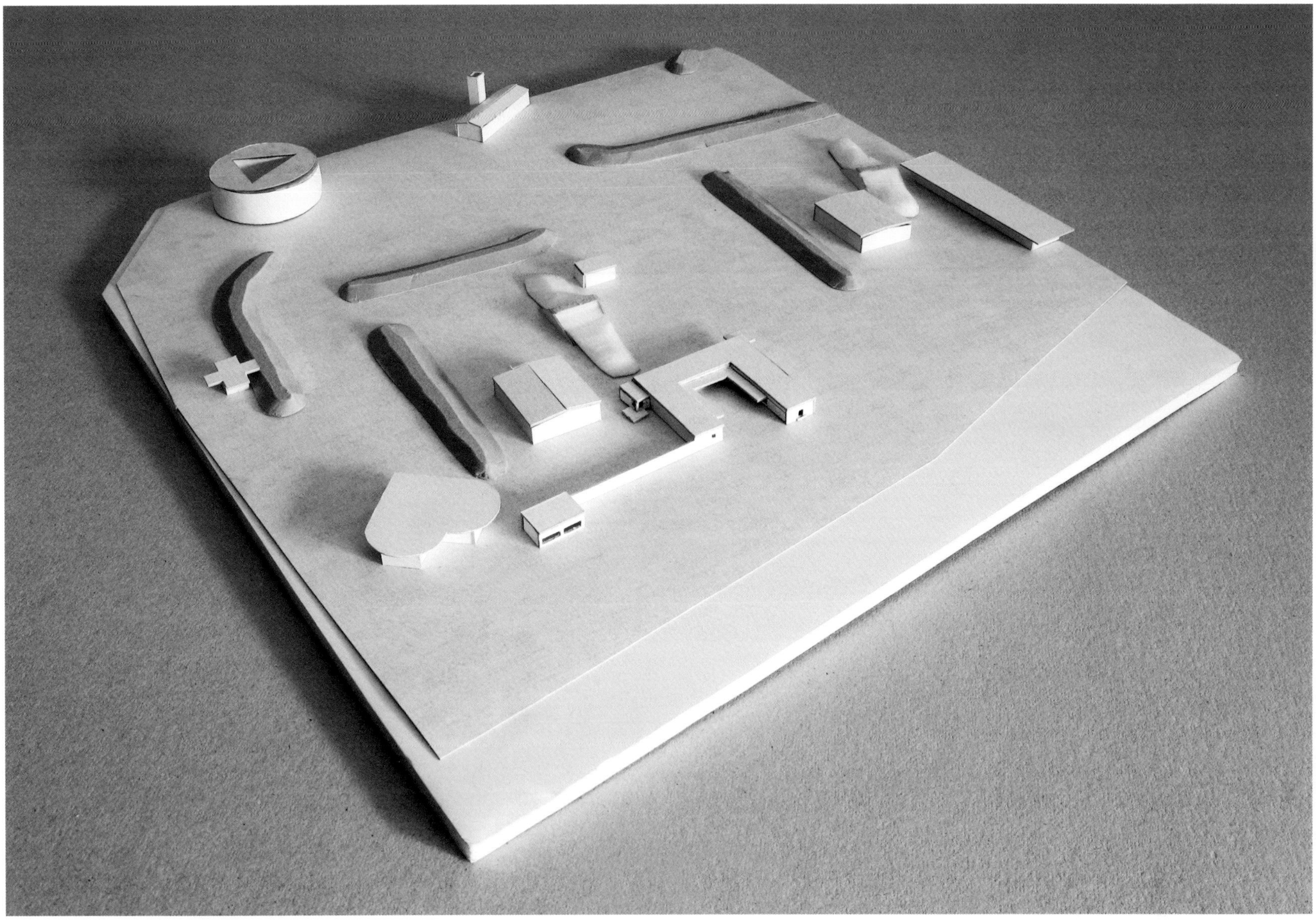

Lageplan / Site plan

Architectural museum Hombroich 27

Innenraumskizzen / Interior sketches

Auditorium / Auditorium

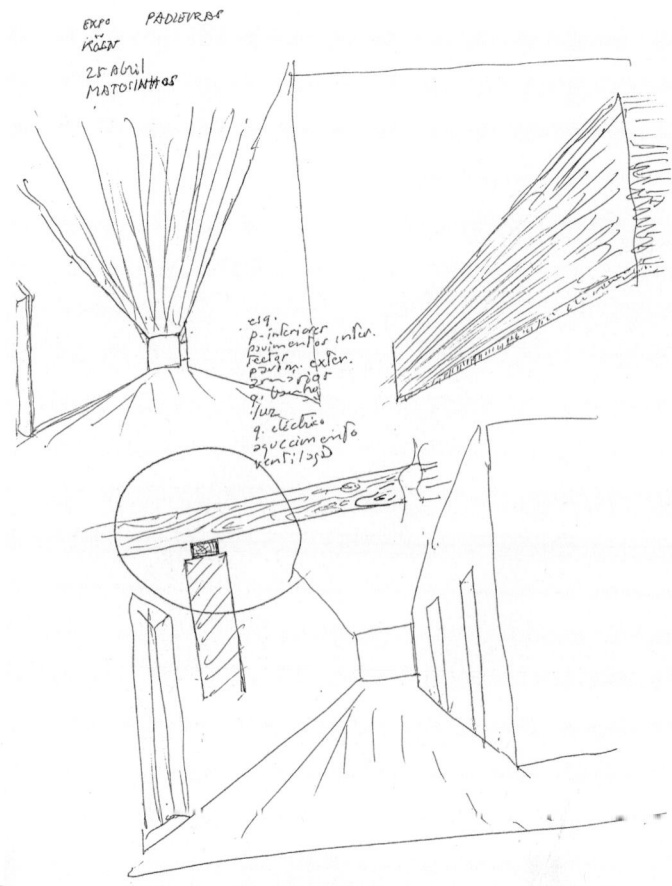

Ausstellungsräume / Exhibition rooms

28   Architekturmuseum Hombroich

Blick durch Ausstellungsräume / View through exhibition rooms

Bad / Bathroom

Innenhof / Courtyard

Fenster zum Hauptraum / Window to main space

Skizze Hauptraum / Sketch of main space

◂ *Fenster zum Hauptraum / Window to main space*

Architectural museum Hombroich

Raumortlabor
städtebauliches Projekt, Insel Hombroich, Deutschland (2005–)
Mit Rudolf Finsterwalder

Spaceplacelab
urbanistic proposal, Insel Hombroich, Germany (2005–)
With Rudolf Finsterwalder

Der Ort   Die vorgeschlagene Bebauung entwickelt sich in einem landschaftlichen Motiv aus der vorhandenen Bebauung der ehemaligen Raketenstation. In einer ringförmigen Komposition ordnen sich die Gebäude zueinander und lassen die Landschaft hindurchfließen. Beziehungen zu Vorhandenem und der Gebäude untereinander formen einen spezifischen Ort.

Die Einpassung   An der Haupterschließung werden die öffentlichen und größeren Gebäude situiert, in den tiefer gelegenen Bereichen zur Autobahn hin werden privatere und kleinere Bauten positioniert. Die höheren Bauten schirmen die kleineren von der Straße ab.

Das Programm   Zwei- bis dreigeschossige Bürobauten bilden den Auftakt der Anlage, das zweigeschossige Hotel öffnet sich zur Landschaft, seine Zimmer blicken in die Weite.   Das High-Tech-Service-Building steht mit seinen zwei Geschossen auf einem Luftgeschoss. In den Wald eingestreut, verteilen sich die Wohnateliers, über einen großen Hof wird das Museum mit seinen sechs Metern Raumhöhe erschlossen. Siebengeschossig ist der Bürobau gegenüber dem Abraham-Bau.

Landschaft   Wie die Bebauung, so lagern sich die Waldzonen um den offenen mittigen Bereich herum. Innerhalb des gesamten Quartiers werden die Flächen durch einen landwirtschaftlichen Betrieb, der sich im Quartier 13 befindet, bewirtschaftet. Eine Tierhaltung in Koppelwirtschaft wird mit einem Anbau von Gemüse kombiniert. Ein Teil der Wiesen wird als Streuobstwiese genutzt.

Place   The proposed settlement uses a landscape concept based on the existing structures of the former missile base. The individual buildings relate to each other within a circular composition, allowing the landscape to pass through them. The buildings' relationships with the pre-existing elements and with each other create a specific place.

Integration   The public buildings are placed along the main access route. More private, smaller buildings are positioned within the lower-lying areas along the motorway. The taller buildings screen the smaller ones from the road.

Program   Two- to three-storey office buildings form the beginning of the complex. The two-storey hotel opens towards the landscape, and its rooms offer views into the distance. The two-storey high-tech service-building stands on piloti.   Residential studios are scattered in the forest. The museum with its 6m tall rooms is accessed via a large courtyard. The office building opposite the Raimund Abraham building is seven storeys high.

Landscape   Both the buildings and the forest are situated around an open field, located at the center. Within the whole Quarter the fields are cultivated by the agricultural company that is located in Quarter 13. A keeping of animals in a paddock system is combined with the planting of vegetables. A part of the fields is also used for fruit trees.

5 Wohnungen
5 Apartments

Skizze Quartier / Sketch of quarter

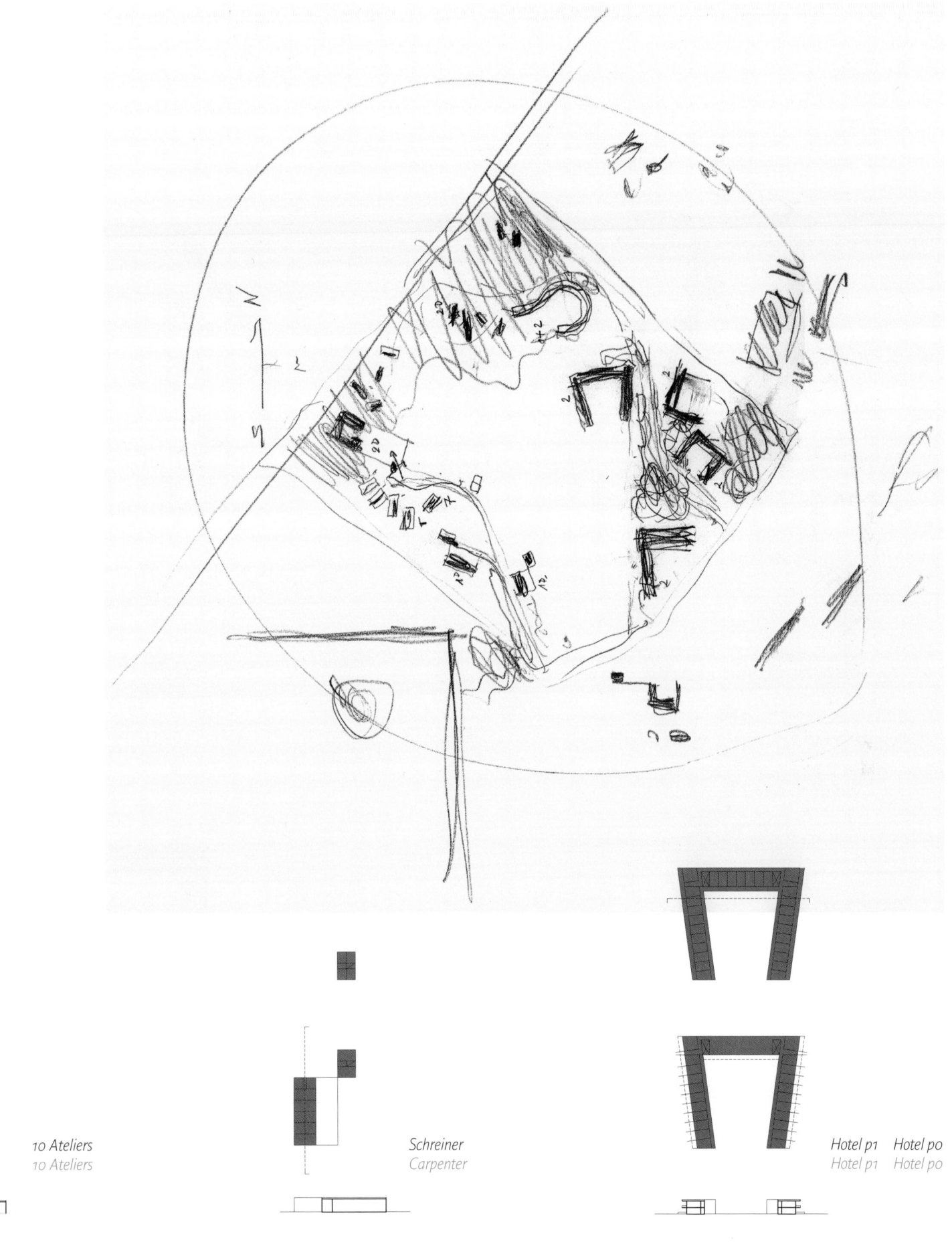

10 Ateliers
10 Ateliers

Schreiner
Carpenter

Hotel p1   Hotel po
Hotel p1   Hotel po

Spaceplacelab

Lageplan / Site plan

1	Bürogebäude (2 Etagen, 3900 m²)	**10**	Schreiner (1/2 Etagen, 432 + 150 m²)	**5**	High Tech Service Building (2 floors, 3454 m²)
2	Bürogebäude (2 Etagen, 2160 m²)	**11**	Steinmetz (1/2 Etagen, 250 + 150 m²)	**6**	10 Ateliers (1/2 floors, 1200 m²)
3	Bürogebäude (2 Etagen, 1680 m²)	**12**	Straße (3570 m²)	**7**	Museum (1 floor, 950 m²)
4	Hotel (2 Etagen, 3702 m²)			**8**	Apartments (1/2 floors, 900 m²)
5	High-Tech-Service-Gebäude (2 Etagen, 3454 m²)	**1**	Office Building (2 floors, 3900 m²)	**9**	Office Building (7 floors, 1400 m²)
6	10 Ateliers (1/2 Etagen, 1200 m²)	**2**	Office Building (2 floors, 2160 m²)	**10**	Carpenter (1/2 floors, 432 + 150 m²)
7	Museum (1 Etagen, 950 m²)	**3**	Office Building (2 floors, 1680 m²)	**12**	Stone Mason (1/2 floors, 250 + 150 m²)
8	Wohnungen (1/2 Etagen, 900 m²)	**4**	Hotel (2 floors, 3702 m²)	**12**	Road (3570 m²)
9	Bürogebäude (7 Etagen, 1400 m²)				

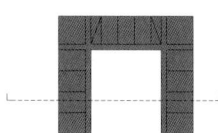

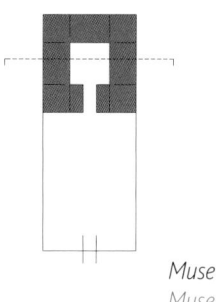

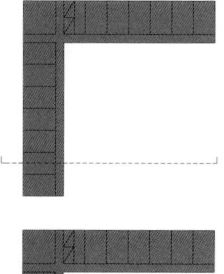

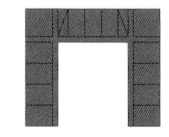

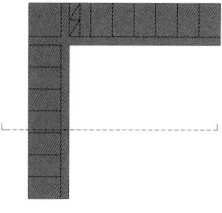

Bürogebäude
Office Building

Museum
Museum

Bürogebäude
Office Building

34 Raumortlabor

Modell Quartier / Model of quarter

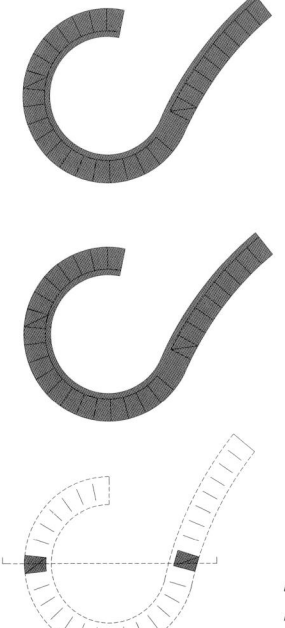

*High-Tech-Service-Gebäude
Erdgeschoss frei*

High Tech Service Building
Ground floor free

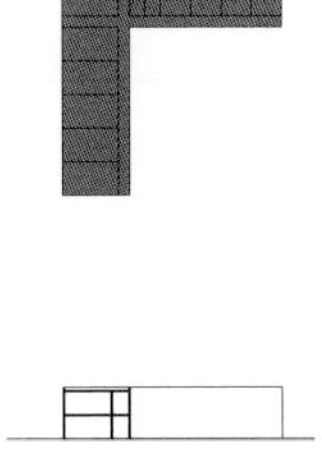

Bürogebäude
Office Building

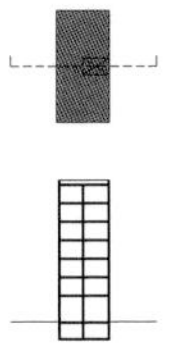

Bürogebäude
Office Building

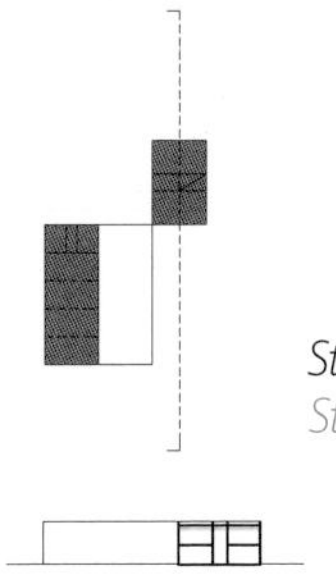

Steinmetz
Stone Mason

Spaceplacelab

Portugiesischer Pavillon
EXPO 2000, Hannover, Deutschland (1999–2000)   **Mit Eduardo Souto de Moura**

Portuguese Pavilion
EXPO 2000, Hanover, Germany (1999–2000)   **With Eduardo Souto de Moura**

Der Pavillon wurde als ein rezyklierbares Ausstellungsgebäude für die EXPO 2000 in Hannover errichtet. Nach der EXPO 2000 wurde er in Coimbra, Portugal, wieder aufgebaut, wo die dortige Stadtverwaltung ihn für Ausstellungszwecke sowie für Konzerte und andere Veranstaltungen nutzt. Das Gebäude stand mitten in einem dieser typischen internationalen Messegelände. Anders als bei der EXPO 1998 in Lissabon, bei der beabsichtigt war, ein Industriequartier zu einem neuen Stadtviertel umzugestalten, wurde in Hannover eine Weltausstellung mit abbaubaren Pavillons, ein Durcheinander an unterschiedlichen Exponaten, von denen einige sehr interessant, andere weniger interessant waren, verwirklicht. In diesem Falle gab es keinen kontextuellen Rahmen. Daher ist das Gebäude ein freistehender Pavillon, welcher nun in einem Park in Coimbra steht. Es war von Anfang an als ein Pavillon im Park konzipiert, mit der Einschränkung, dass es sich bei der EXPO 2000 um einen Park voller Pavillons handelte.

Der Eingangshof wird von einem L-förmigen Baukörper umgeben. Der größte Innenraum ist auch gleichzeitig die Ausstellungshalle. Die Dachlandschaft ist wellenförmig, hat etwas Organartiges und ist in Form einer doppelten, künstlichen Hülle hergestellt. Tageslicht kann hierdurch einfallen, zugleich dient die doppelte Haut dem Wärmeschutz und stellt im Inneren gute akustische Bedingungen her. Außen ist der Pavillon hauptsächlich mit Kork, ein Teil der Fassade mit portugiesischen Fliesen, den so genannten *azuleijos*, verkleidet. Der kompaktierte Kork garantiert Langlebigkeit für den Außenbereich und ist in seiner Erscheinung eine ungewöhnliche Wärmeisolierung. Der rohe, dunkle Kork verändert seine Farbe mit der Zeit zu einem Grau; wir werden sehen, wie er sich entwickelt.

The Pavilion is an exhibition hall built for EXPO 2000 in Hanover that is dismountable in order to be re-useable. It has now been re-erected in Coimbra, and the local city council intends to use it for exhibitions, concerts, etc. The building was located at the centre of one of those typical international fairs. But, unlike the EXPO in Lisbon — where there was a purpose and a plan to transform the area into a new urban zone —, in Hanover there was a World Fair with dismountable pavilions, a jumble of different items on display, some of which were very interesting, others far less so. Thus, in this case, there was no planned contextual relationship. As such, the building is an independent pavilion, now located in a park in Coimbra. From the outset it had been a pavilion in a park, except that the initial park housed a mass of other pavilions. The Pavilion has an 'L' shape, around the access patio. The largest volume is the main exhibition room. The roof covering is undulated, has an organic shape, and is made in the form of a double synthetic screen, in order to enable light to enter while providing thermal insulation and creating good acoustic conditions. On the outside, the Pavilion is mainly covered in cork with a section covered in *Azulejo* tiles. The agglomerated cork covering guarantees durability for the exterior and constitutes an unusual-looking form of thermal insulation. The raw, dark cork will turn grey over time; we shall see how it will evolve.

Nordfassade / North facade

Skizzen des Daches / Sketches of roof

Pavilion Expo Hannover

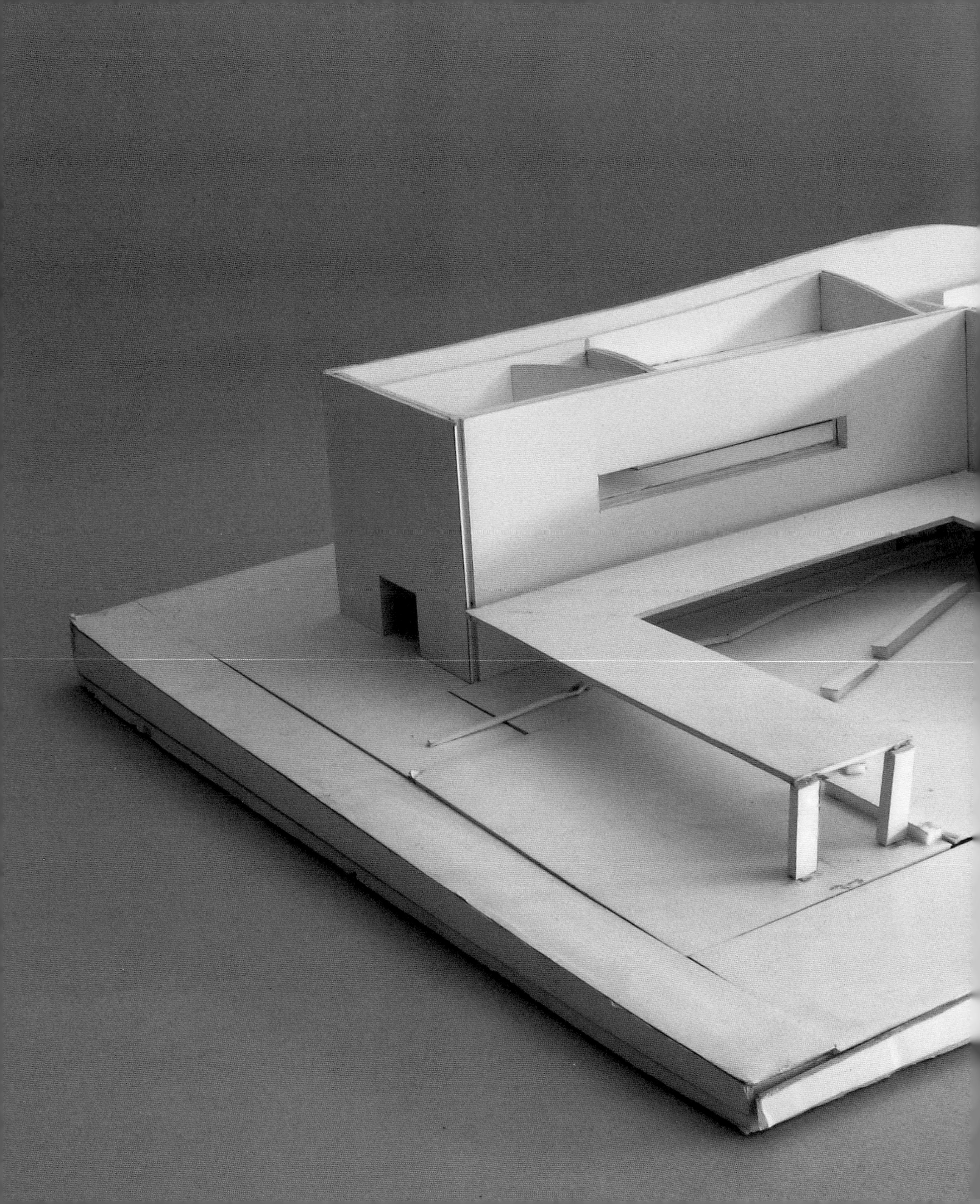

Offenes Modell / Open model

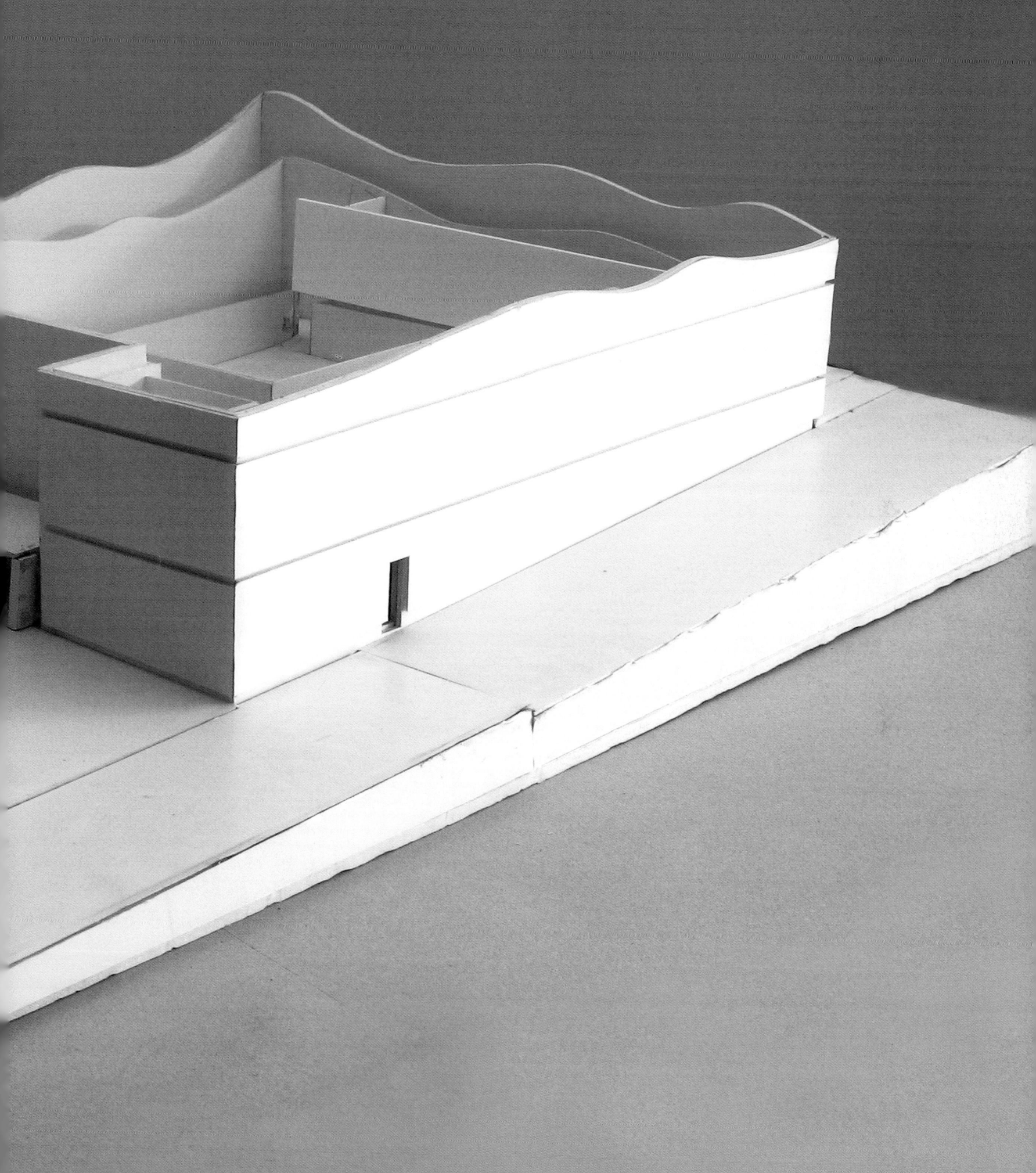

Decke / Ceiling

Haupttreppe / Main staircase

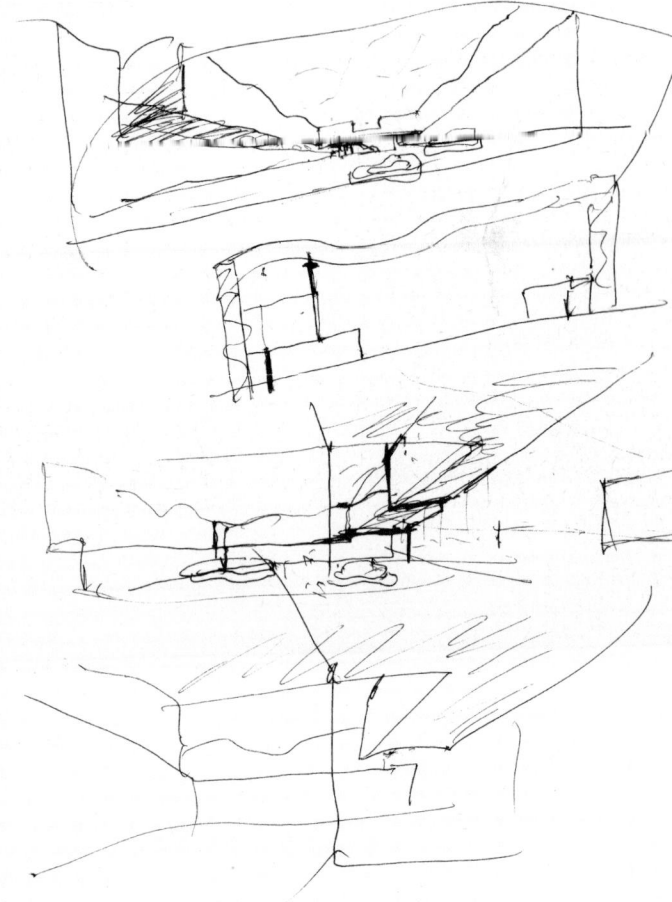

Skizzen Ausstellungsfläche / Exhibition space sketches

40 Pavillon Expo Hannover

Haupteingang / Main entrance

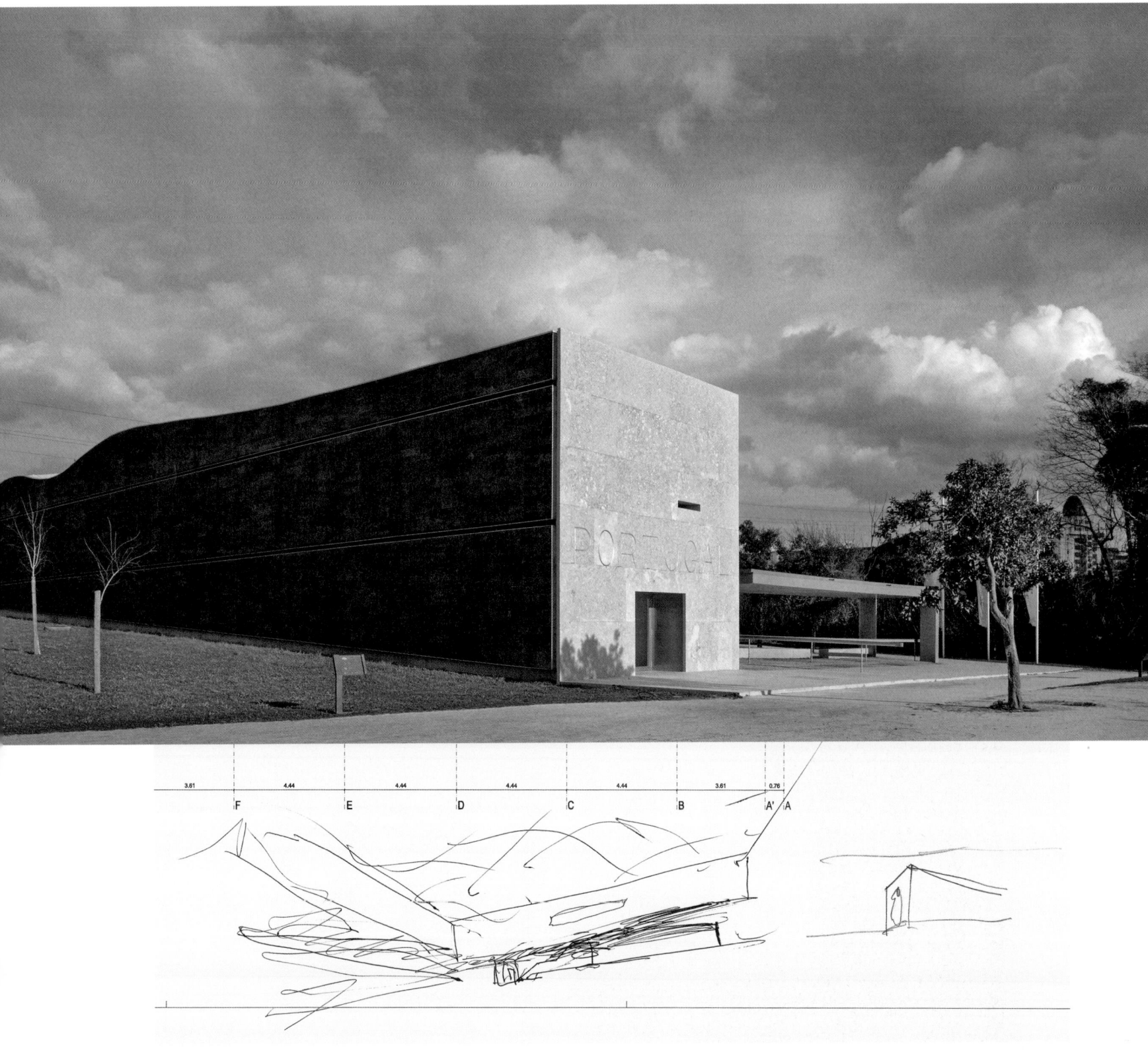

Skizze Decke / Ceiling sketch

Pavilion Expo Hannover   41

Hof / Courtyard

1	Halle	**10**	Lift	**1**	Hall	**10**	Lift
2	Ausstellungshalle	**11**	Lager	**2**	Exhibition Hall	**11**	Storage
3	Shop	**12**	Lager	**3**	Shop	**12**	Storage
4	Coffee-Shop	**13**	WC	**4**	Coffee-Shop	**13**	WC
5	»Cybercafe«	**14**	Abfallentsorgung	**5**	"Cybercafe"	**14**	Waste Disposal
6	Halle Vip	**15**	Technikraum	**6**	Hall Vip	**15**	Technical Room
7	Lager	**16**	Brandmeldeanlage	**7**	Storage	**16**	Fire alarm system
8	Lager			**8**	Storage		
9	Lager			**9**	Storage		

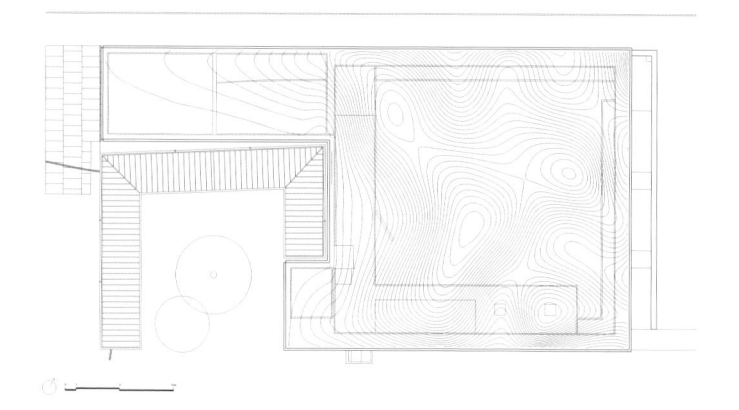

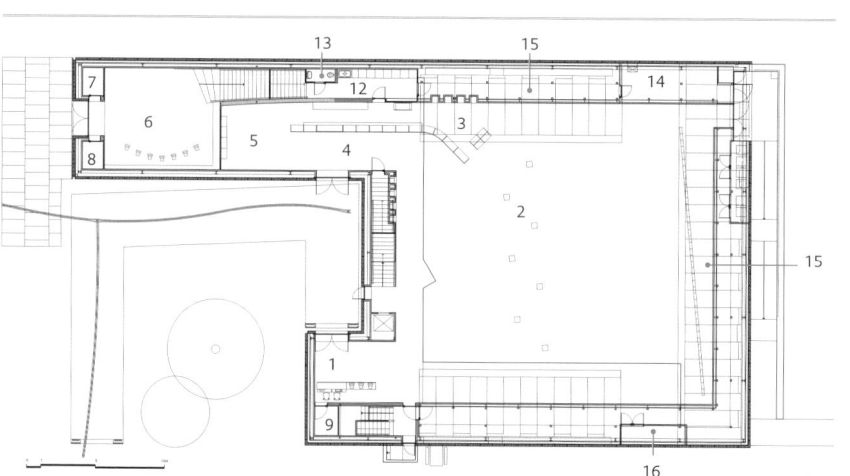

Dachaufsicht und Grundriss Erdgeschoss / Roof plan and ground floor plan

Offenes Modell / Open model

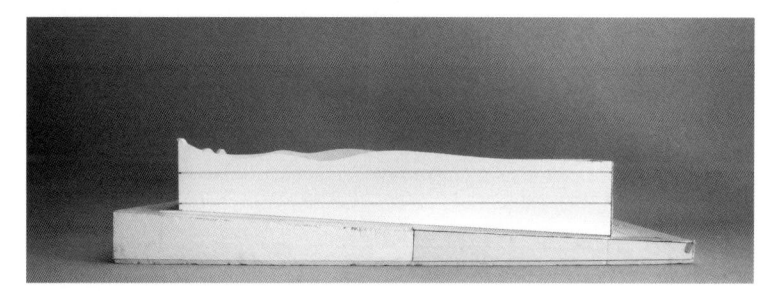

Dachlinien Modell / Roof line model

Studien / Studies

Pavilion Expo Hannover

Iberê Camargo Stiftung
Porto Alegre, Brasilien (1998–2009)

Iberê Camargo Foundation
Porto Alegre, Brazil (1998–2009)

Der Hauptzweck für dieses Gebäude war die Errichtung eines Gebäudes zur Unterbringung der Sammlung des bekannten brasilianischen Malers Iberê Camargo. Die Witwe des Malers verfolgte den Entwurfsprozess mit großem Enthusiasmus und tatkräftiger Unterstützung, eine Sponsorengruppe garantierte die Existenzfähigkeit des Museums. Die Stadt Porto Alegre bot das Grundstück an — ohne jegliche Vegetation und mit einem Steilhang, der von einem ehemaligen Steinbruch resultierte.   Bezüglich seiner Größe ist das Grundstück relativ klein, schmal und grenzt an eine dicht befahrene Straße. Vom Grundstück erstreckt sich ein exquisiter Blick über den Fluss Guaíba — einen jener südamerikanischen Flüsse, die so aussehen, als wären sie das Meer. Das Museum musste als vertikaler Bau entwickelt werden. Über drei Ebenen erstrecken sich Ausstellungsräume und in einem verbundenen Anbau befindet sich ein Atelier für Unterrichts- und Ausbildungszwecke. Das zu lösende Hauptproblem betraf die Frage, wie man die Bedürfnisse des Museums mit einem derart schmalen Grundstück in Einklang bringen und gleichzeitig die Parkplatzfrage lösen konnte, für die es auf dem Grundstück nicht genügend Fläche gab, da der Keller bereits für das Archiv, Lagerräume und einen kleinen Vortragssaal vorgesehen war. Die vorgeschlagene Lösung, bei der ich befürchtete, dass sie verworfen werden würde, die aber dann doch angenommen wurde, sah den Bau einer unterirdischen Garage unter der Straße selbst vor. Der Baukörper spiegelt die Wellenform des Steilhangs wider. Die Schauseite des Gebäudes ist ebenfalls wellenförmig gehalten, sozusagen symmetrisch zum Hang. Der Innenraum ist durch eine große, zentrale Halle geprägt, die von Räumen in einer L-förmigen Anordnung umsäumt ist. Ein durchgehender Gang führt sowohl nach oben als auch nach unten, mittels Treppen, Aufzügen und Rampen. Die Höhenunterschiede zwischen den Geschossen werden durch eine Rampe überwunden, die sich teils innen und teils außen befindet, also vom eigentlichen Körper des Baus losgelöst.

The main aim of this programme was to construct a building in order to house the collection of Iberê Camargo, a well-known Brazilian painter. The artist's widow followed the design work with great enthusiasm and support, and a group of sponsors guaranteed the museum's viability. The land was offered by the Porto Alegre municipality — with no vegetation cover and a very steep slope, corresponding to a former stone quarry.

The site is relatively small in size, narrow and bordered by a busy avenue. The view is exquisite, looking over the Guaíba River — one of those South American rivers that look as if they are the sea. The museum had to be developed as a vertical construction. There are three floors of exhibition rooms and also an atelier for teaching and apprenticeship in interconnected annexes. The main difficulty that had to be faced was to harmonize the museum's needs with such a narrow plot of land, and to resolve the problem of parking given that there was no land available, since the basement was used for archives, storage and a small auditorium. The proposed solution, which I feared would be rejected but was actually approved, was to build the car-park below the avenue itself. The form of the building mirrors the undulated shape of the slope against which it is built. The front of the building is undulated in a symmetrical manner to the slope itself. The interior is characterized by a large central space, with rooms around it, forming an 'L' shape. There is a continuous walkway leading up and down, achieved via steps, lifts, and ramps. The height differences between the floors is resolved through a ramp that is partially on the inside and partially on the outside, thus detached from the volume of the building itself.

Eingangsfassade / Entrance facade

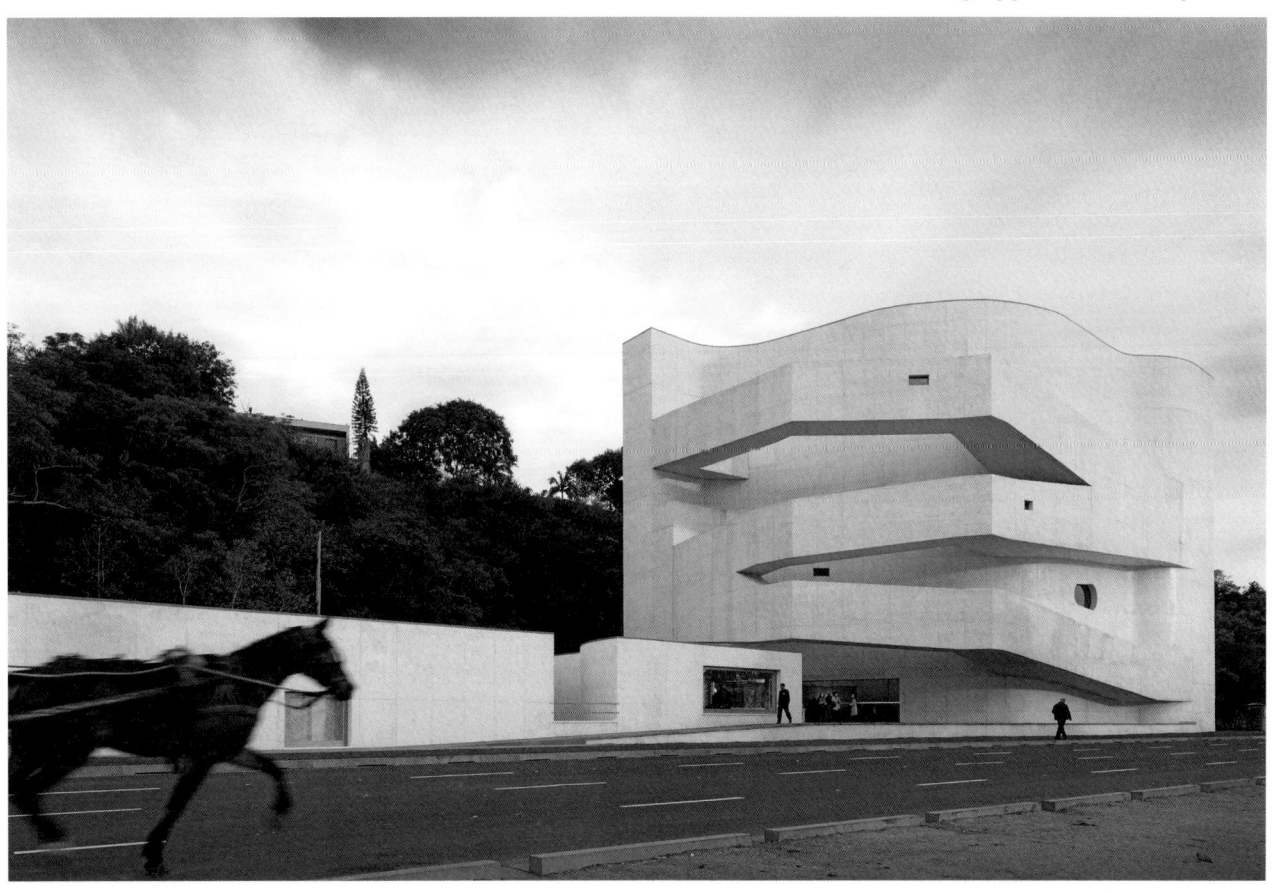

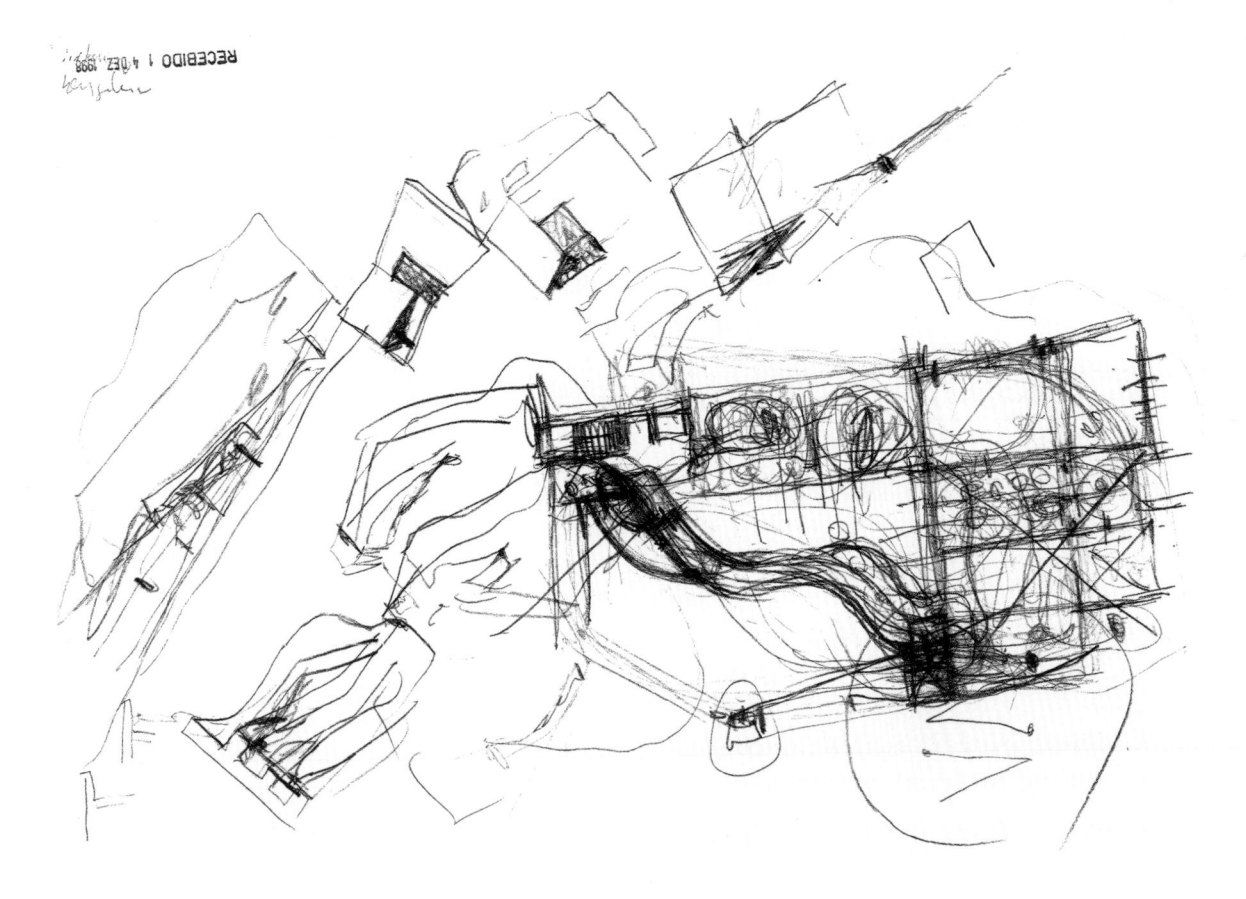

Gesamtkonzept / Overall scheme

Museum Iberê Camargo

Innenhof / Courtyard

Rampen / Ramps

Volumenstudie / Volume study

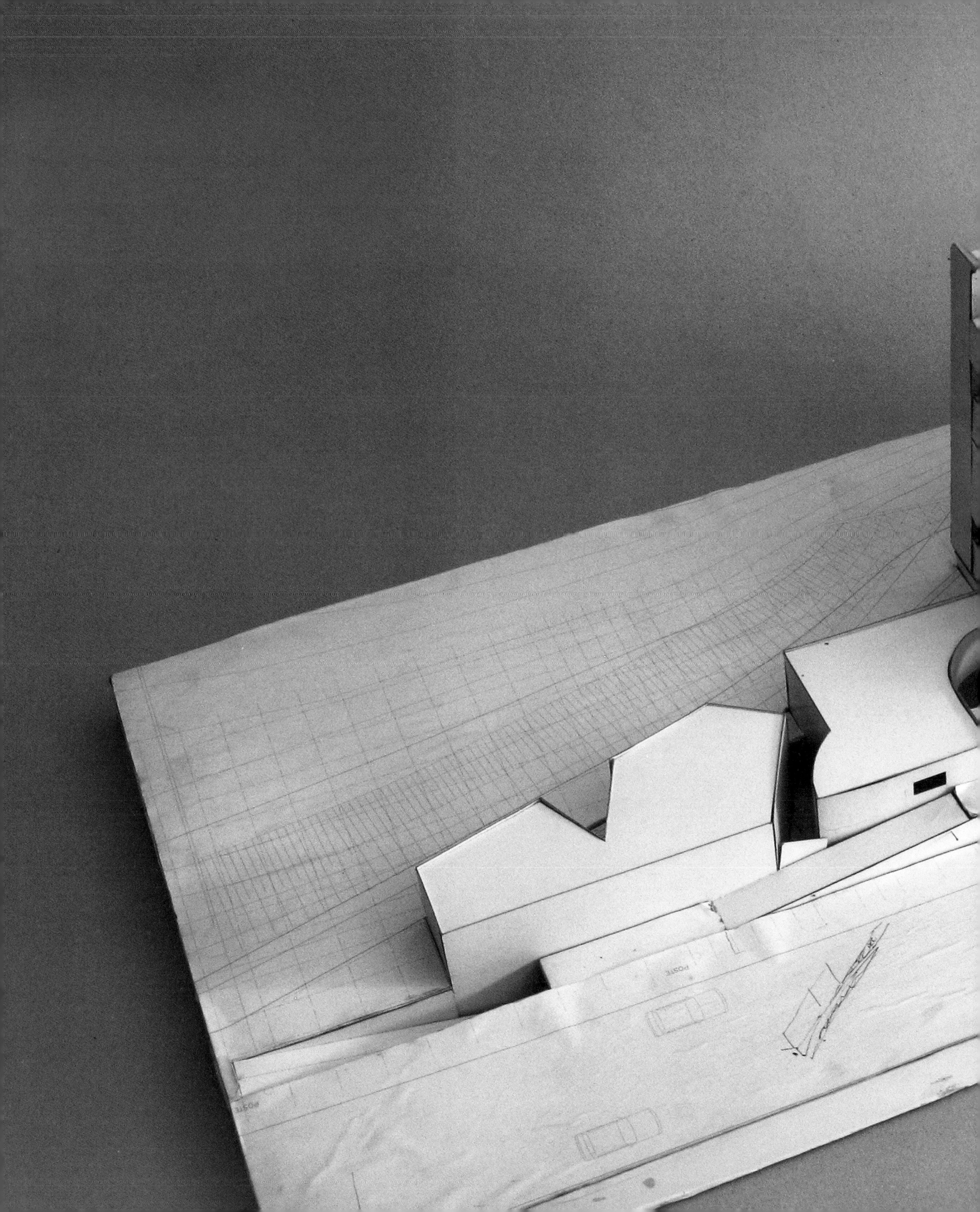

Gesamtmodell / Complete Model

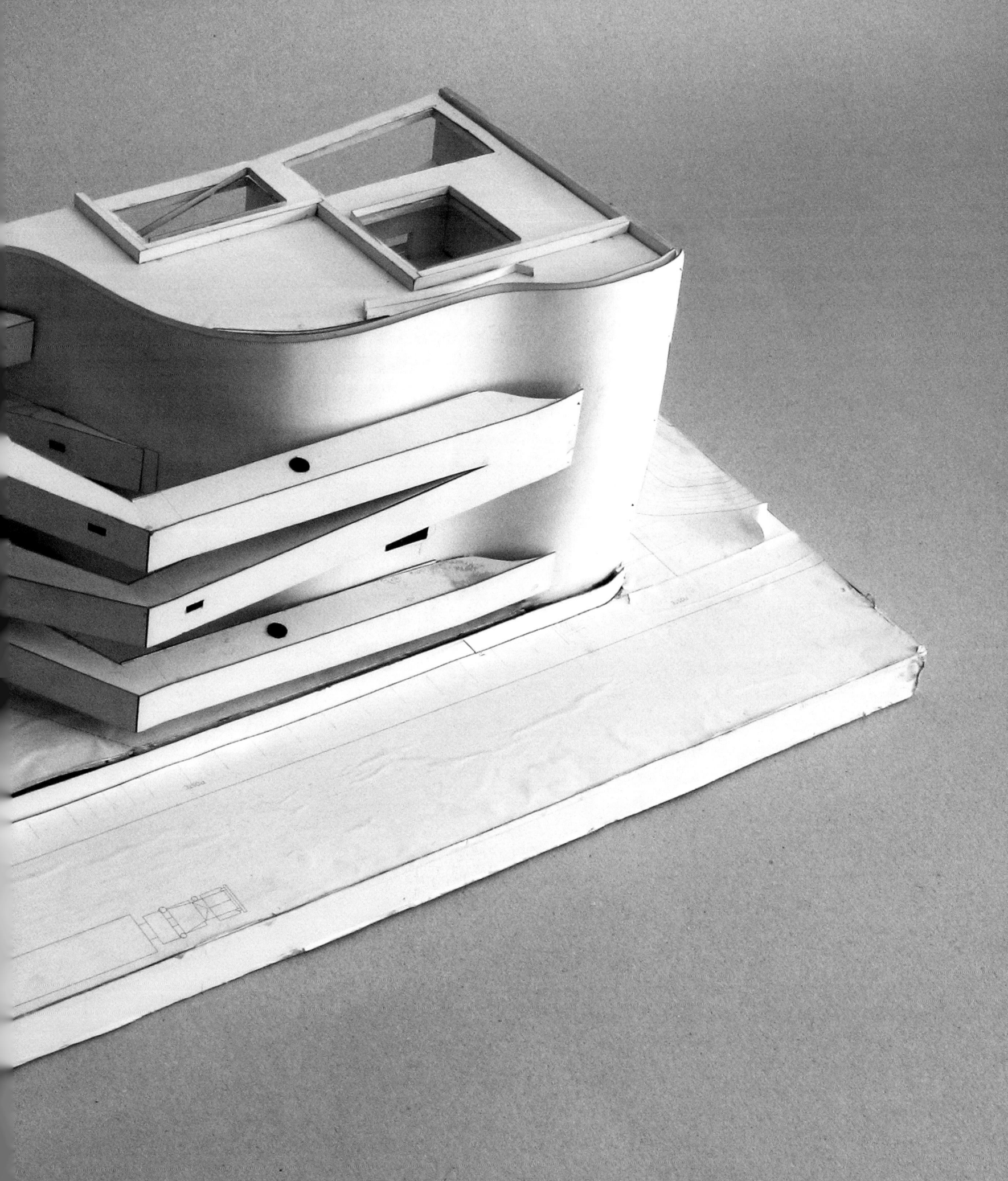

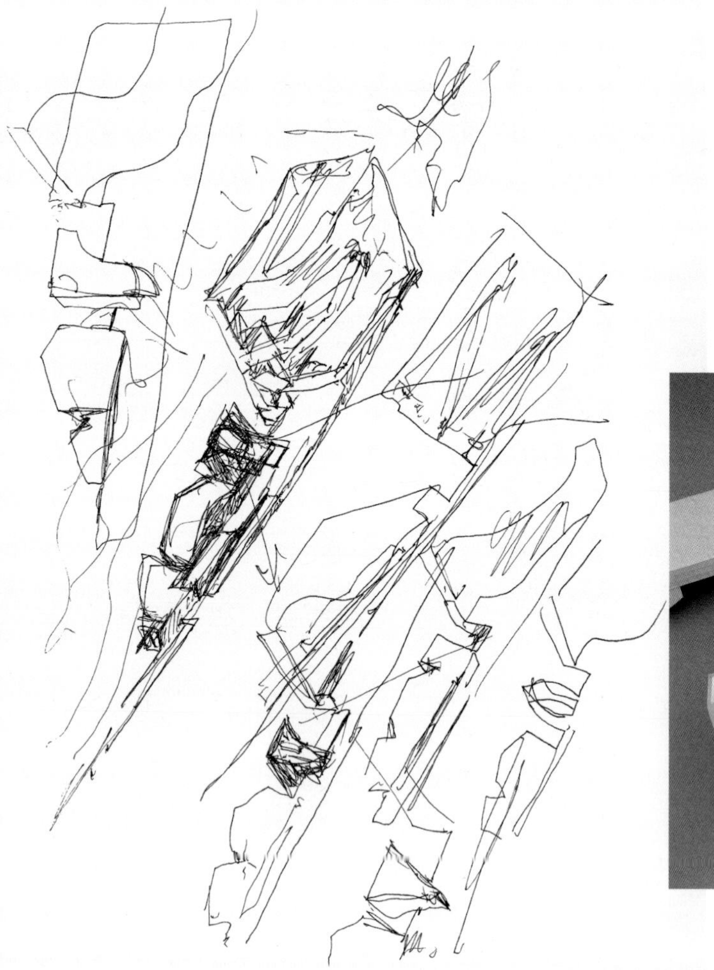

Studien / Studies

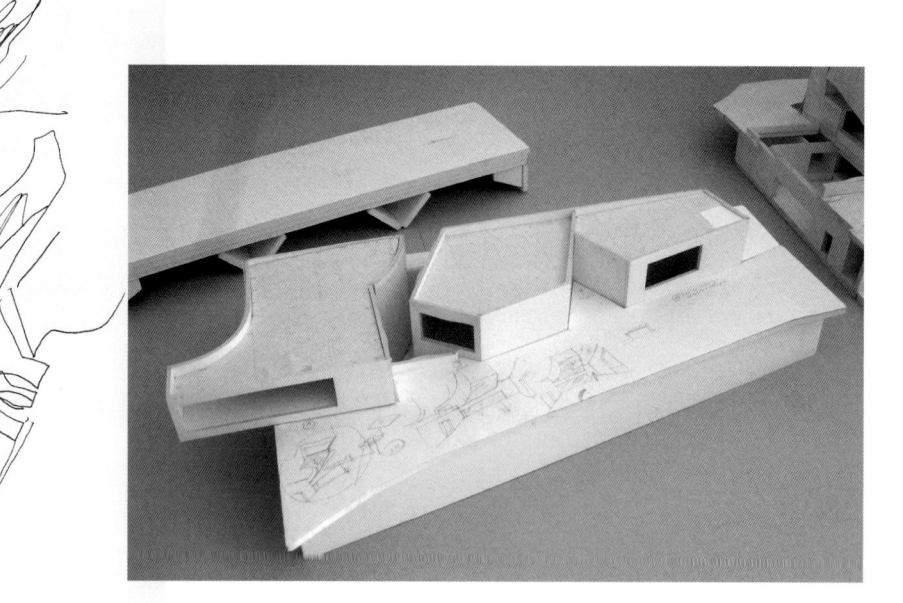

Teilmodell / Partial model

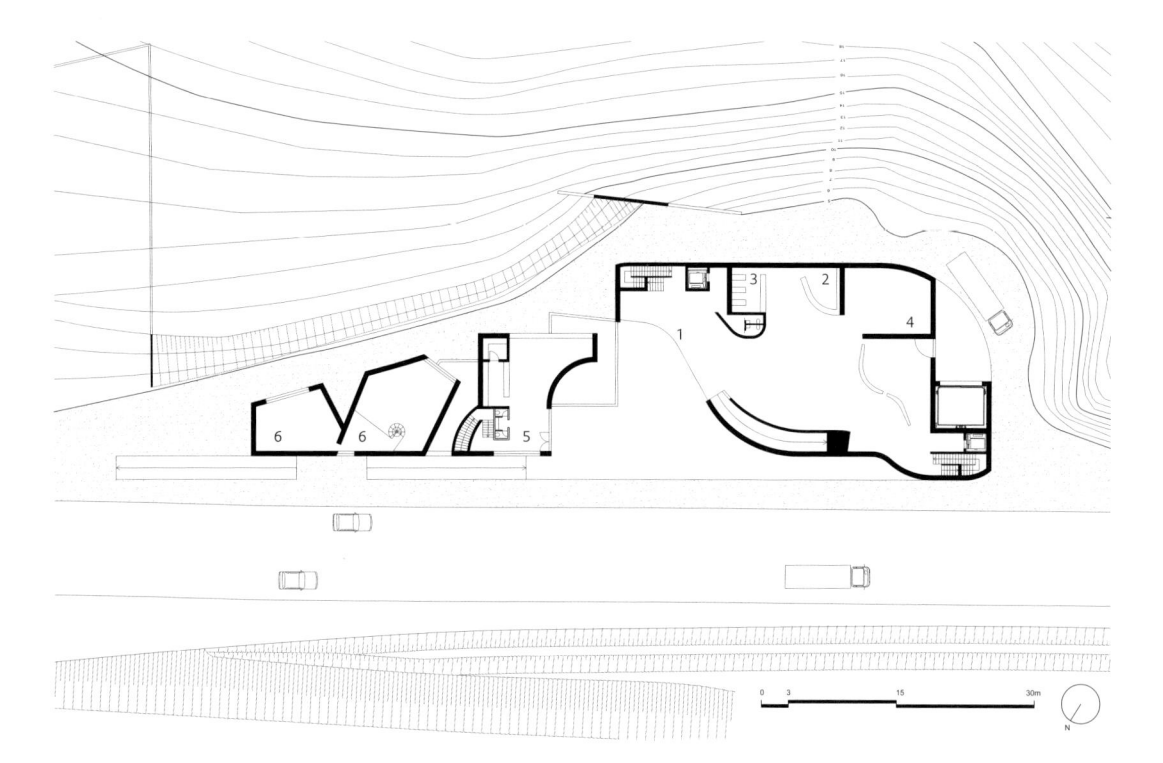

1	Eingang
2	Empfang
3	Garderobe
4	Buchhandlung
5	Imbiss
6	Künstler Werkstatt

1	Entrance
2	Reception
3	Closet
4	Book Store
5	Snack-Bar
6	Artistic Workshop

Grundriss Erdgeschoss / Ground floor plan

Museum Iberê Camargo

Eingang im Modell / Entrance in the model

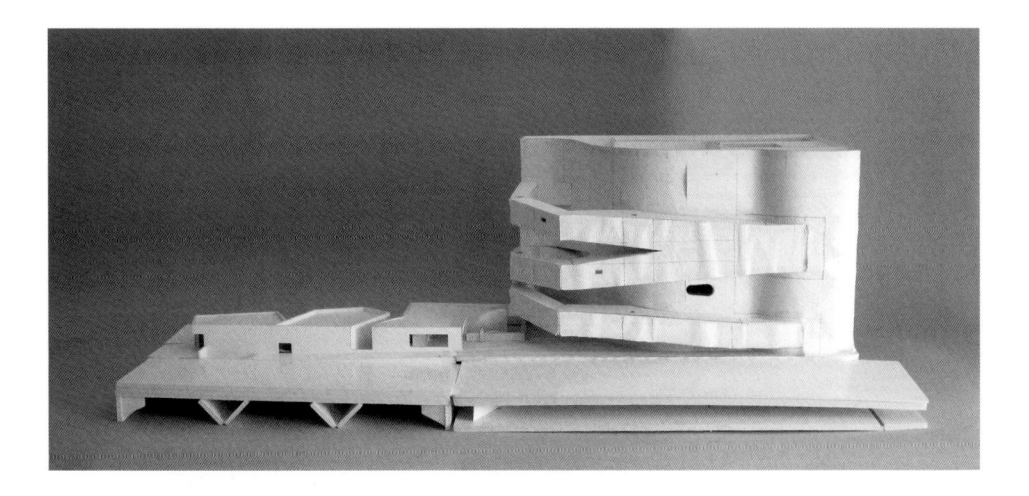

Museum Iberê Camargo

Innen-Außen / Interior-Exterior

Foyer / Foyer

Rampe / Ramp

Museum Iberê Camargo

Ausstellungsraum / Exhibition room

Auditorium / Auditorium

Museum Iberê Camargo

Ausstellungsräume / Exhibition spaces

Ausstellungsräume / Exhibition spaces

Lichthof / Atrium

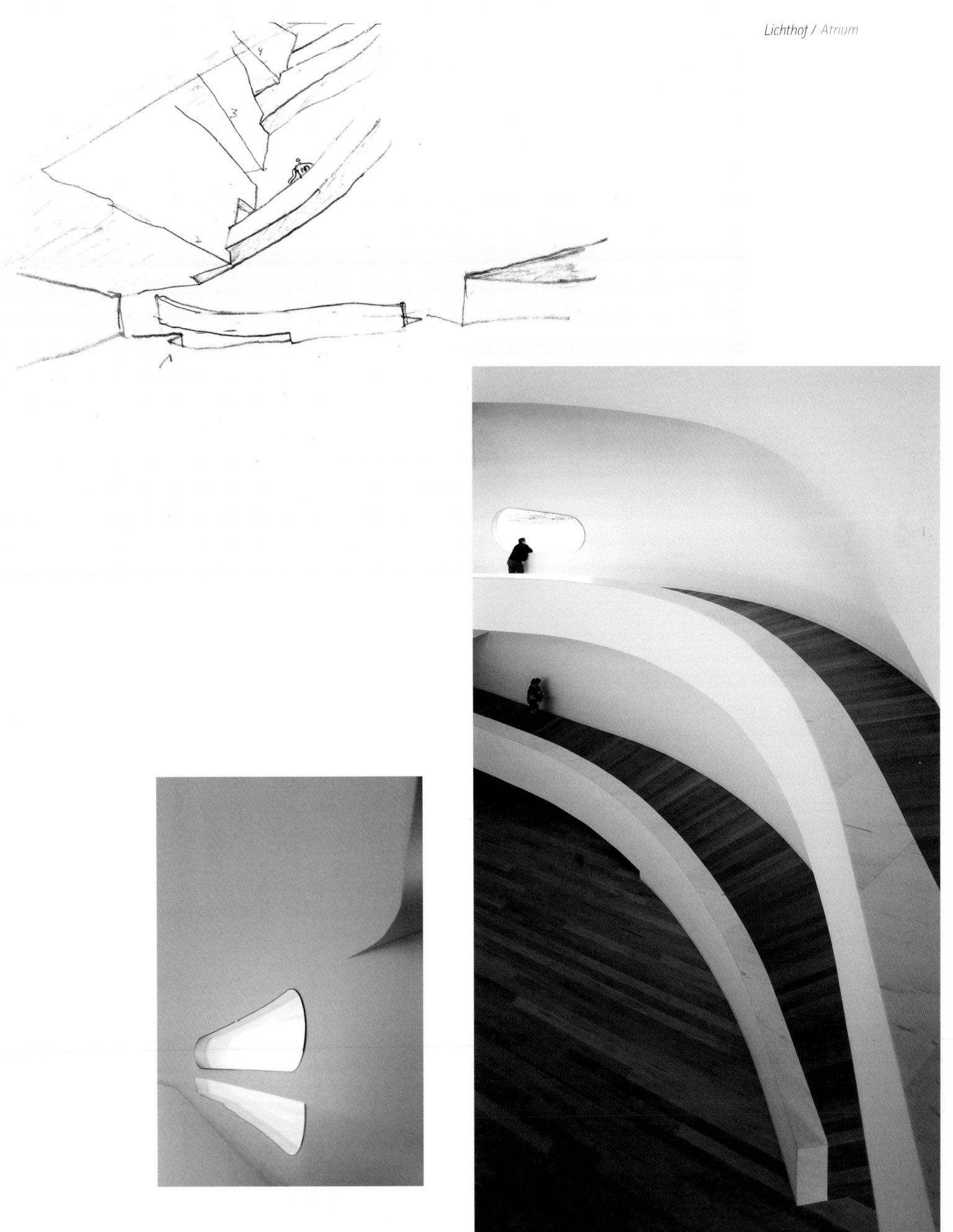

Rampen / Ramps

Kirche Santa Maria
Marco de Canavezes, Portugal (1990–1996)

Church Santa Maria
Marco de Canavezes, Portugal (1990–1996)

Das Raumprogramm dieser katholischen Kirche für eine ländliche Gemeinde ist auf drei zweistöckige Bauten aufgeteilt: Gebäude A mit der Kirche und Aussegnungshalle, Gebäude B mit dem Saal und den Räumen für die Sonntagsschule und Gebäude C mit der Wohnung für den Pfarrer.

Der Kirchengrundriss besteht aus einem einfachen rechteckigen Kirchenschiff von 30 m Länge. Der Haupteingang liegt am südwestlichen Ende. Der Altar wird durch die konvex abgeschliffenen, inneren Ecken des Kirchenschiffs charakterisiert. Er ist 45 cm vom Fußboden des Langhauses angehoben und wird quer unterhalb der konvexen Form in einer Deckenhöhe von 5 m geführt. Im Kirchenschiff haben 400 Gemeindemitglieder Platz; es wird durch drei in die gekurvte Form der tiefen Nordwestwand eingeschnittene große Öffnungen im Bereich der Decke, ein horizontales Streifenfenster entlang der südöstlichen Wand, einen Lichtschacht hinter dem Altar, welcher auch die Aussegnungshalle mit Tageslicht versorgt, und die zeremoniellen Eingangstüren beleuchtet.

Die Taufkapelle am Haupteingang bildet sich nach außen hin ab. Die andere Projektion wird als alltäglicher Eingangsbereich zur Kirche benutzt und nimmt auch die Treppe zu Orgelraum und Glockenspiel auf. Ein rechtwinkliger Nebenbau enthält den verbreiteten Teil des Altars, die Sakristei, das Standesamt und die Beichträume. Eine Treppe und ein Aufzug stellen eine Verbindung zur Aussegnungshalle im Untergeschoss her.

The program of this Catholic Church for a rural parish is distributed among three two story buildings: building A with the church and mortuary chapel, building B with the auditorium and Sunday school, and building C with the priest's house. The new buildings are arranged to compliment the existing built environment and together make a ceremonial space in front of the church door.

The plan of the church is a simple rectangular nave 30 m long. The main entrance is at the south-west end of the nave. The altar is characterized by the erosion of the nave's internally convex corners. It is raised 45 cm above the level of the nave floor and extends laterally under the convex form with a lower ceiling height of five meters. The sanctuary seats 400 and is illuminated by three large openings cut into the curved form of the deepened north-west wall at the ceiling level, a continuous horizontal opening along the south-east wall, a light shaft behind the altar that also illuminates the mortuary chapel below, and the ceremonial entrance door to the church.

The baptistery, at the main ceremonial entrance, occupies one of the projecting volumes of the façade. The other volume acts as a lobby to the everyday side entry of the church and contains the access stair to the organ and bells. A subsidiary rectangular form lies to one side of the nave and contains the lateral extension of the altar, the sacristy, the registry, and the confessional rooms. A stair and elevator connect these spaces to the mortuary chapel below.

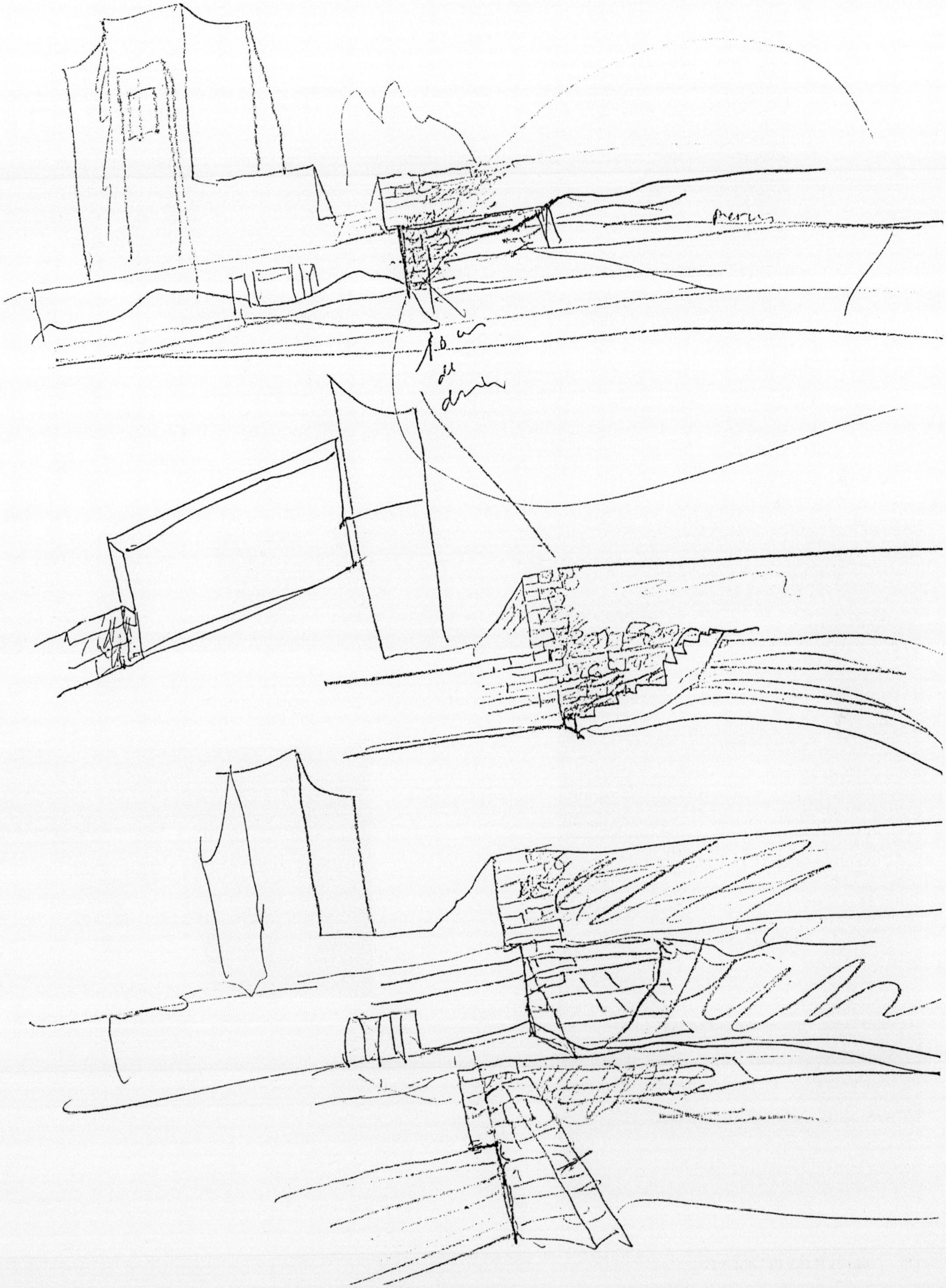

Gesamtmodell / Site model

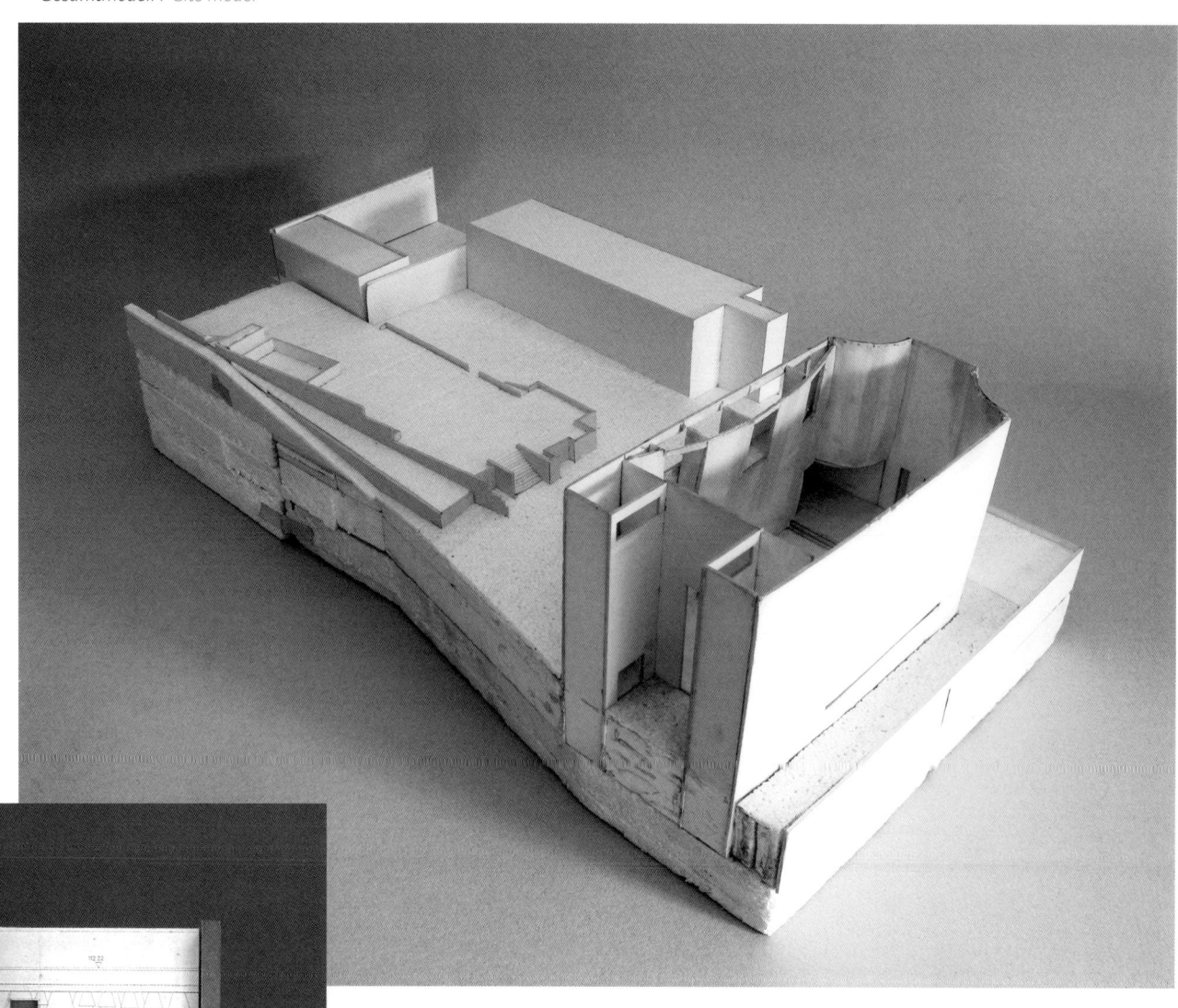

Treppenturm / Staircase

58 **Kirche Marco de Canavezes**

Nordost-Fassade / Northeast facade

Innenraumstudien / Interior studies

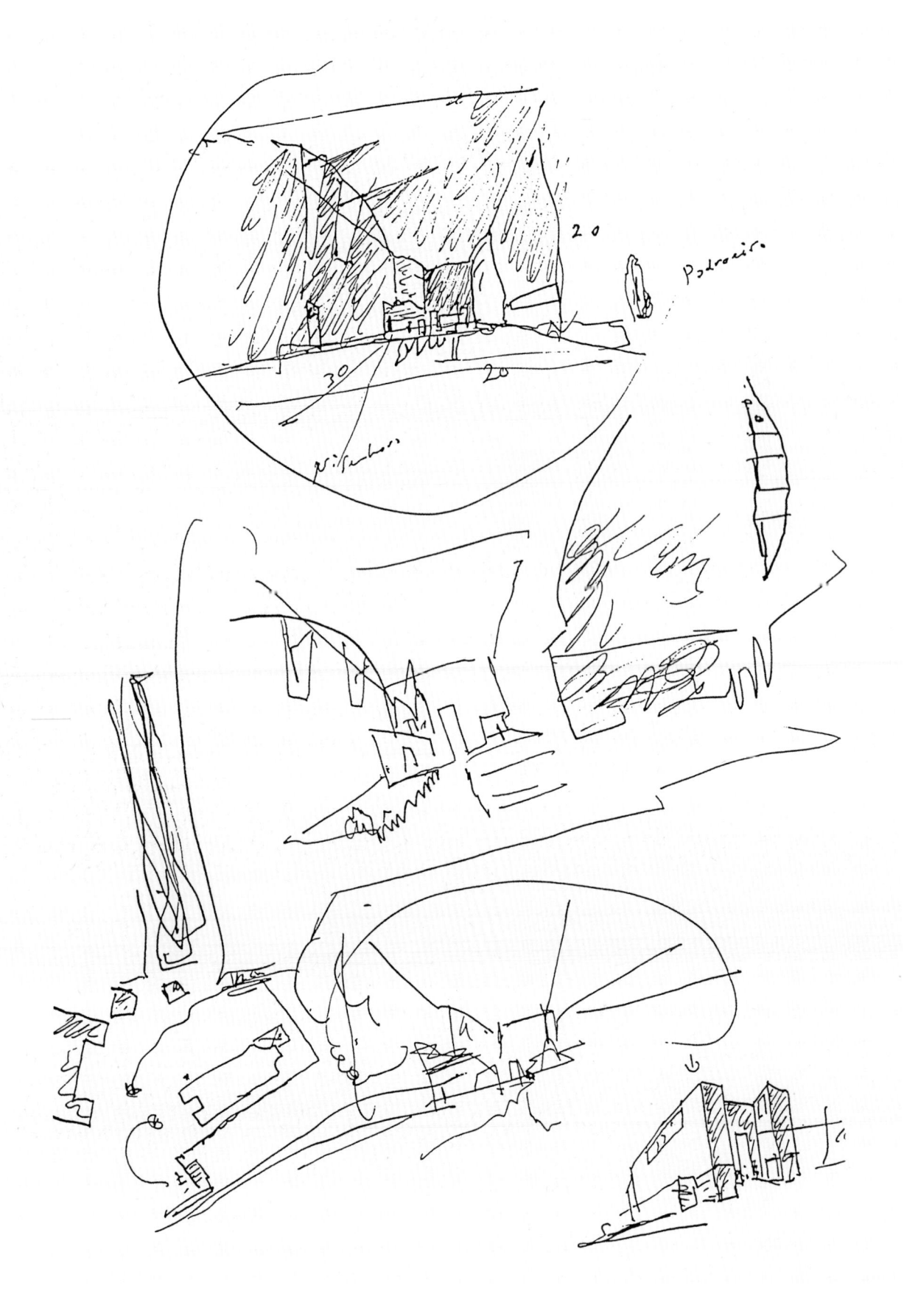

60 Kirche Marco de Canavezes

Geländemodell / Site model

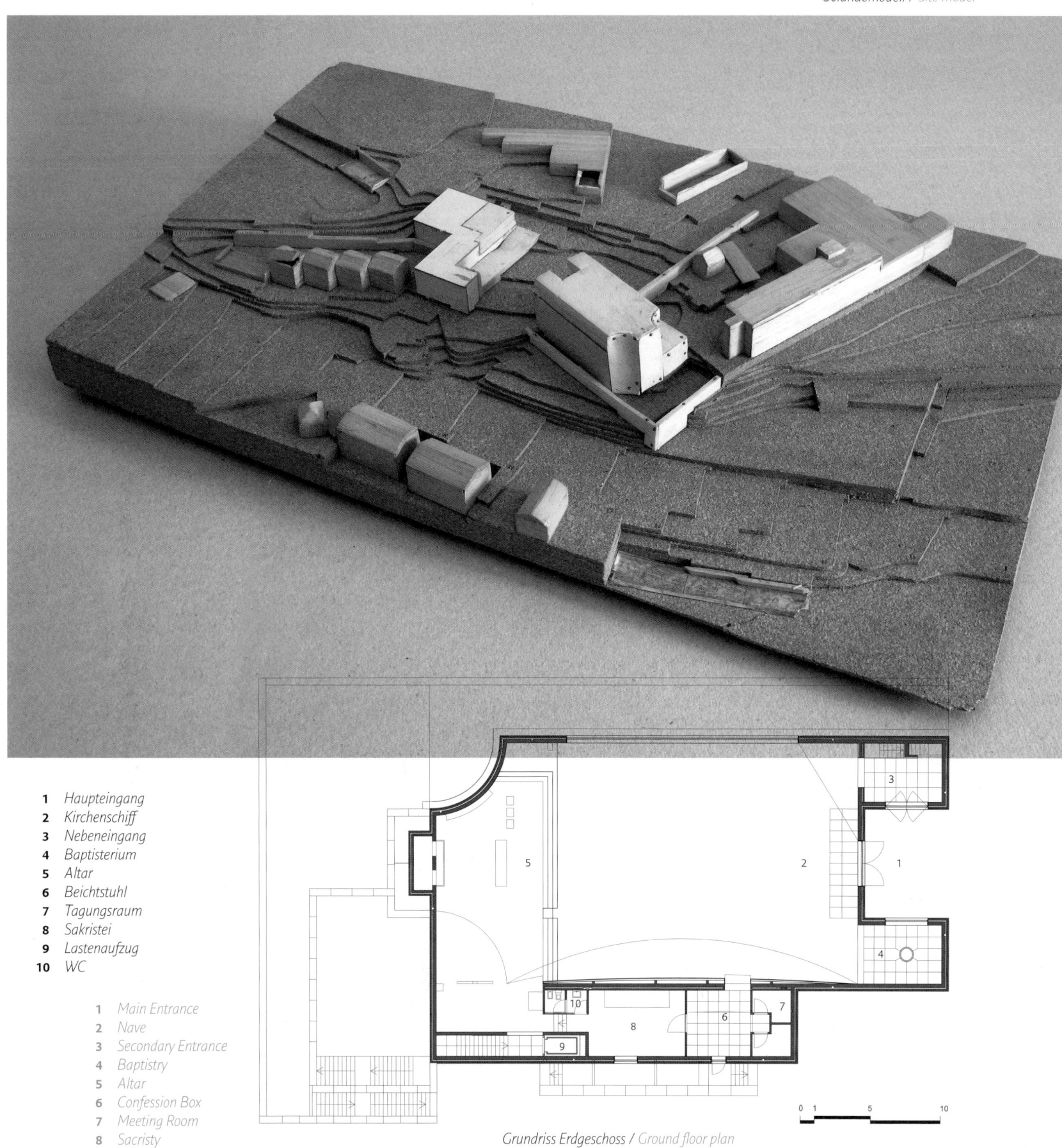

1	Haupteingang
2	Kirchenschiff
3	Nebeneingang
4	Baptisterium
5	Altar
6	Beichtstuhl
7	Tagungsraum
8	Sakristei
9	Lastenaufzug
10	WC

1	Main Entrance
2	Nave
3	Secondary Entrance
4	Baptistry
5	Altar
6	Confession Box
7	Meeting Room
8	Sacristy
9	Service Lift
10	WC

Grundriss Erdgeschoss / Ground floor plan

Church Marco de Canavezes

Nave und Altar / Nave and Altar

Eingangstür / Entrance door

Licht von oben / Light from above

Innen-Außen / Interior-Exterior

Gespräch Rudolf Finsterwalder mit Álvaro Siza
am 3. März 2011

Conversation Rudolf Finsterwalder with Álvaro Siza
on March, 3rd 2011

Da wir in der geplanten Ausstellung in Hombroich Arbeitsmodelle und Skizzen zeigen wollen, möchte ich Sie fragen, welchen Einfluss diese Medien auf Ihre Arbeit haben.

Die Skizze ist die schnellste und einfachste Form der Kommunikation, mit sich selbst und den Mitarbeitern. Sie erlaubt ein sehr schnelles Ausprobieren von Ideen, sie ermöglicht eine Untersuchung von Formen und manchmal führt sie zu Antworten auf Probleme, gelegentlich fast intuitiv. Alvar Aalto hat darüber einen kleinen Text verfasst, der besagt, dass es manchmal vorkam, als er in einem Projekt oder einem Problem feststeckte und nicht weiterkam, dass er sein Skizzenbuch nahm und zeichnete, ohne an das Problem zu denken. Manchmal ist es dann passiert, dass aus den Zeichnungen zufällig etwas entstand, das ihm für sein Projekt eine entscheidende Idee gebracht hat. Vor allem deshalb zeichne auch ich und natürlich auch, weil es mir Spaß macht. Das Modell erlaubt eine komplette Kontrolle und erlaubt mir eine Kontrolle aus der Distanz, wenn ich nicht vor Ort sein kann. Wie z.B. im Fall von Korea, da haben wir sehr große Modelle gebaut, die ich betreten konnte, und so konnte ich alles kontrollieren und besprechen. Wenn ein neues Projekt kommt, machen wir erst einmal ein Umgebungsmodell mit der Topografie und dann eine Studie der Volumen, begleitet von vielen Skizzen, und danach größere Modelle, alles begleitet vom Computer. Eine Entwicklung, eine Untersuchung geschieht mit Hilfe dieser Mittel, auch mit der Genauigkeit des Computers. Der Einsatz von CAD hat viel verändert: Wenn man mit der Hand gearbeitet hat, geschah es in Phasen, aber wenn du es im Computer zeichnest, muss es sehr genau sein, ein Computer abstrahiert nicht, ist nicht ungenau. Was wir einen Vorentwurf genannt haben, ist praktisch nicht mehr möglich, da es, wegen der großen Genauigkeit, ein direkter Übergang in die Ausführungsplanung ist. Das ist ein gravierender Wandel im Rhythmus der Arbeit und die Zusammenarbeit im Team hat sich dadurch sehr verändert.

As we want to show in the Hombroich exhibition working models and sketches, I want to ask you what impact these media have on your work.

The sketch is the easiest and simplest way of communication, with oneself and with the colleague. It allows a very quick study of ideas, an investigation of forms and sometimes leads to answers on problems, sometimes it happens spontaneously. Alvar Aalto wrote a short text about that phenomenon which says, that sometimes it happened that he was stuck in a project or a problem and couldn't go ahead, he left it and started to draw or paint without thinking about it. Sometimes it happened that, casually, something grew out of his drawings that helped him to solve the problem. That's the reason why I sketch and because of course I enjoy it. To work with models allows complete control and monitoring from a distance, when I cannot be on the site. As in the case of Korea, we built huge models that I could move in and control and discuss everything. When a new project starts, we first build a model of the surrounding with the topography and then a study of the volumes, accompanied by many sketches and then larger models, all accompanied with the computer. A revelation, an investigation always is done with these media, even with the precision of the computer. The use of CAD has changed a lot. When one worked by hand it happened in phases, but when one works with the computer it must be very precise, a computer cannot be abstract, it is not inaccurate. What we called a pre-study is no longer the same, because of the high precision; it is a direct link to the final drawings. This is a profound change in the rhythm of work and the collaboration in the team has also changed a lot.

I also believe that the work has changed a lot because of the computer, a "try and error", or "I like it, I like it not" mentality has prevailed.

If the work is accompanied with sketches and models it can be effective. I myself cannot run a computer but of course all the people in my office can.

Ich glaube auch, dass die Arbeit mit dem Computer viel verändert hat, ein »try and error«, ein »I like it, I like it not« hat sich durchgesetzt.

Wenn die Arbeit von Modellen und Skizzen begleitet ist, um ein Projekt zu entwickeln, so funktioniert das. Ich selbst kann einen Computer nicht bedienen, aber in meinem Büro arbeiten alle mit dem Rechner.

Ich möchte über etwas sprechen, was sehr wichtig für Ihre Arbeit ist, die »implantação«, ein Wort, das im Deutschen oder Englischen keine Entsprechung hat und das Einfügen eines Gebäudes in seine Umgebung bezeichnet.

Wenn man sich mit einem Ort auseinandersetzt, so engt er zum einen ein, zum anderen gibt er Anregungen, ein Projekt zu entwickeln.

Mit dem Begriff ist auch das Finden der richtigen Höhen gemeint.

Es war zum Beispiel bei unserem Wettbewerbsentwurf für die Alhambra sehr schwierig, da die Topografie sehr bestimmend und sehr komplex war. Das ganze Terrain war abschüssig, es bestand aus Rampen und Terrassen. Auch die Wahl des Ortes war schwierig und überdies gab es nicht sehr viele Möglichkeiten, sondern der Ort war vorgegeben und es war mehr eine Frage des Wie als des Wo.

Frank Lloyd Wright hat auch eine ähnliche Idee von organischer Architektur, einer intensiven Beziehung zur Natur und zur Landschaft, organisch aber auch in einem strukturellen Sinne, dass alle für die Architektur relevanten Themen bedacht und in ein Projekt integriert wurden.

Es ist kein additives Denken, sondern ein integratives. Frank Lloyd Wright hat eine Serie von Gebäuden in einer horizontalen Landschaft entworfen, die sich alle um einen Kern entwickeln, den Herd, den Mittelpunkt des Hauses. Von ihm ausgehend, strecken sich Gebäudeteile wie Arme in die Landschaft. Es ist interessant, dass auch Mies van der Rohe dieses Prinzip anwandte, wenn auch in sehr unterschiedlicher Weise.

I want to talk about something very important to your work, the "implantação", a term that has no equivalent in German or English and means inserting a building into its surroundings.

When you deal with a site, it restricts you on the one hand but on the other it is a stimulation to develop a project.

This term also means the search for the right heights.

As in our competition project for the Alhambra it was very difficult, because the topography was very decisive and complex. The whole terrain was very steep; it consists of ramps and terraces. Even the choice of the site was difficult and overall there weren't many choices because the site was defined and it was more a question of how and not where.

Frank Lloyd Wright had a similar idea of organic architecture, an intense relationship to nature and landscape, organic also in a structural sense, so that all relevant themes would be considered and integrated in a project.

It is not an additional thought, but an integral one. Frank Lloyd Wright had developed a series of buildings in a horizontal landscape that are all organized around a core, the stove, the center of the house. From this starting point the building elements spread out like arms in the landscape. It is interesting that also Mies van der Rohe was working with the same principle, even if they are very different architects.

In one of your texts you write about your relationship to nature and declare that you want to set a counterpoint, not to imitate nature. This is maybe more a Miesian position, although, Frank Lloyd Wright at the end of his career also introduced vertical and futuristic elements into his work.

In einem Ihrer Texte schreiben Sie über Ihr Verhältnis zur Natur und erklären, dass Sie einen Kontrapunkt setzen, nicht die Natur nachahmen wollen. Das ist vielleicht mehr eine Mies'sche Position, obwohl Frank Lloyd Wright am Ende seiner Schaffensperiode auch vertikale und futuristische Elemente in seine Arbeit einführte.

Mir scheint, er hat seine Haltung nicht geändert, er hat einfach an Orten gearbeitet, die eine andere Reaktion erforderten, z.B. in einem Gebäude, das man von oben betritt und das sich nach unten entwickelt, sehr zum Unterschied von den Gebäuden in einer flachen Landschaft, den »Prairie Houses«. Dort ist es die Horizontalität, die dominiert, und das ergibt die komplette Verschiedenheit gegenüber Orten mit einer vertikalen Topographie. Ich sehe das in der gleichen Linie, aber sehr unterschiedlich in der Ausprägung, seine sehr intelligente Form, auf die verschiedenen Voraussetzungen zu reagieren.

Ich glaube, in Ihrem Werk ist es sehr speziell, dass Sie in einem kleinen Land wie Portugal geboren sind und jetzt in vielen Teilen der Erde Projekte realisieren. Das Gleichgewicht zwischen dem authentischen, sehr eigenen Herangehen und der Auseinandersetzung mit den verschiedenen Orten und Aufgaben erscheint mir sehr fruchtbar.

Ich habe kein sehr gutes abstraktes Vorstellungsvermögen, also muss ich einen griffigen Ansatz zur Entwicklung eines Projektes finden. Das ist mein persönlicher Ansatz, an den verschiedenen Orten muss es ein jeweils unterschiedlicher und spezifischer Zugang sein.

In meinen Augen gibt es viele Architekten Ihrer Generation, deren Entwicklung sich in einem Stillstand befindet, die sich wiederholen. In Ihrer Arbeit jedoch hat man das Gefühl, dass sie sich beständig weiterentwickelt, immer mit einer klaren Handschrift, aber auch immer wieder neu.

Der Grund ist das Fehlen von Vorstellungskraft, ich muss meine Augen öffnen, um zu sehen, wo ich arbeite.

I think he didn't change his ideas; he just worked on sites that wanted a different kind of reaction. For example in a building that one enters on the top and then emerges at the bottom, this is very different from the houses on a flat landscape, the Prairie houses. There it is horizontality that dominates and it is completely different from sites with a vertical topography. I see this continuity of thought, even in projects that appear quite different, demonstrating his intelligent way of reacting to different circumstances.

I think in your oeuvre it is very special, that you were born and have grown up in a small country like Portugal and now realize projects in many parts of the world. The balance between the authentic, very personal way of working and the struggle with the various locations and tasks seems very successful to me.

I don't have a good imagination, so I have to find a proper approach to the revelation of a project. This is my personal idea; on the different sites there must be a different and specific approach.

In my opinion there are many architects of your generation that repeat their own architecture. But in your work, I have the feeling that there is a constant development, always with a clear signature, but always new.

The reason is the lack of imagination; I must open my eyes to see where I am working.

For me it is interesting to see the development of your idea of space, from beginning with simple interior spaces arising more and more complex spatial concepts.

This is because there is a holistic idea of inner and outer space, a linkage, with a mutual influence. For me the clearest architecture in this sense is by Adolf Loos. I remember when I hardly knew him, and didn't like his work, it seemed strange, like when he worked with doors

Für mich ist es interessant, die Entwicklung Ihres Raumverständnisses zu sehen, wie aus anfänglich einfachen Innenräumen immer komplexere und interessantere Räume und Raumkonzepte entstehen.

Das kommt von einer gesamtheitlichen Idee von Innen- und Außenraum, eine Verflechtung, die sich wechselseitig beeinflusst. Für mich ist die klarste Architektur in diesem Sinne die von Adolf Loos. Ich erinnere mich, als ich ihn kaum kannte, dass er mir kaum gefiel, er kam mir sehr merkwürdig vor, wie er z.B. Fenster und Türen setzte, sehr wirr. Aber dann, mit der Zeit, hatte ich einen anderen Zugang. Ich sah ein sehr individuelles Konzept, es erschien mir nicht diskutierbar, es musste so sein. Nachdem es mir zuerst völlig unregelmäßig erschienen war, sah ich nun eine andere Vorstellung von Ordnung, wie ein Magnetismus, der alle Teile anzog und ordnete. Später, als ich einige seiner Werke besuchte, sah ich, die Klarheit seiner Vorstellung vom Außenraum hing vom Impuls seiner Idee der Organisation des Innenraumes ab, und begriff, wie eines vom anderen abhing und wie sich alles fast magisch in eine unglaubliche Ordnung und Schlüssigkeit verwandelte.

Le Corbusier sagte: »Architektur ist das Spiel der weißen Körper unter dem Licht der Sonne« — sind Sie mit diesem Satz einverstanden?

Das ist ein Aspekt der Architektur. Le Corbusier hat viel in Manifesten gesprochen, so erscheint es manchmal wie ein absolutes Konzept, aber das ist nicht der einzige Ansatz zur Architektur. Er hatte definierte Themen, die er für unverzichtbar hielt, obwohl sie nicht besonders vertieft waren, er hat sozusagen in Fragmenten gesprochen. In seiner Arbeit gibt er eine Art Synthese all dieser Ideen, selten illustrieren jedoch seine Arbeiten seine Ideen.

Das Licht ist sehr wichtig in Ihrer Arbeit, in den meisten Ländern spielt es keine große Rolle — wie können Sie es kontrollieren, vor allem in so komplexen Räumen?

and windows. But later on I had a different idea, I saw an individual concept, not debatable, it had to be like it was. After I thought about it I saw a different idea of organization, like a magnetism attracting all parts and organizing them. Later when I had visited some of his projects I saw that the clarity of his outer space depended on the impulse of his idea from the organization of the inner space; how one thing depended on the other and how everything was almost magically transformed in an unbelievable order and clarity.

Le Corbusier said: "Architecture is the game of the white cubes under the light of the sun". Do you agree?

This is only one aspect of architecture. Le Corbusier talked a lot in manifestos, so it sometimes seems like an absolute concept, but it's not the only approach to architecture. He had certain themes that he thought were indispensable, even if they weren't very well developed, he spoke in fragments. His work is a kind of synthesis of all these ideas, but rarely do his works illustrate his ideas.

Light is very important in your work. How do you manage to control it, especially in such complex spaces?

I told you that it works with the help of these large-scale accessible models. They are indispensable because I can control everything, all relevant aspects. Today, architecture has become very complex, even the light, ventilation, etc., and all relevant rules have to be considered and integrated. It's a union of machinery, planners, officials, etc., and if one doesn't control the relationships between each profession, it can get out of control. If you pass a project to an engineer they exceed with the requirements for ventilation and other technical necessities. To avoid that, I am working in a team in which I steadily try to control the project as a whole. But it really became hard to create a convincing space, with all the subjects and rules. It is definitely essential, from the very beginning, to work in a team and not parallel with individual specialists.

Ich habe ja gesagt, mit diesen großen Modellen, in die ich hineinkann. Sie sind unersetzlich, da ich so alles kontrollieren kann, alle Aspekte, die eine Rolle spielen. Heute ist Architektur sehr komplex geworden, auch das Licht, die Lüftung, und vor allem die Vorschriften müssen bedacht und integriert werden. Es ist eine Union von Maschinen, Planern, Behörden usw., die, wenn man sie und ihre Beziehung untereinander nicht kontrolliert, außer Kontrolle geraten. Wenn man ein Projekt weitergibt, an einen Ingenieur, dann übertreiben sie mit den Anforderungen an Lüftung und in anderen technischen Belangen. Um so etwas zu verhindern, arbeite ich in einem Team, mit dem ich ständig versuche, das Projekt in seiner Gesamtheit zu kontrollieren. Es ist wirklich schwer geworden, einen überzeugenden Raum zu schaffen, mit all den Themen und Vorschriften. Es ist von Anfang an entscheidend, dass man in einem Team arbeitet und nicht nebeneinanderher mit einzelnen Spezialisten.

Das ist wieder wie bei Frank Lloyd Wright, der alle Belange zusammendachte und zusammenführte.
Glauben Sie, es gibt Länder, in denen es schwieriger ist, gute Architektur zu realisieren, z. B. Deutschland?
Ja, auf jeden Fall, je weiter ein Land entwickelt ist, desto schwieriger ist es. Die Beziehung zur Industrie erzeugt diese Vielzahl von Verpflichtungen. In jedem Projekt ist es eine Herausforderung, ein Gleichgewicht zu finden.

Ich glaube, Hombroich war ein wichtiges Beispiel, um zu zeigen, dass es auch in Deutschland möglich ist, so eine Art von Architektur zu erzeugen.
Ja, hier gab es eine große Freiheit in jeder Beziehung. Gebäude wie die bestehenden zu sehen, inmitten eines fantastischen Gartens und gefüllt mit außergewöhnlicher Kunst, ist ein Glücksfall, die Türe zu öffnen zu solchen Gebäuden und nicht die üblichen Überwachungskameras, Lüftungsauslässe usw. zu sehen.

Again that is like Frank Lloyd Wright, who thought and brought all items together. Do you think that in some countries it is more difficult to realize good architecture, such as Germany?
Definitely, the further a country is developed the more difficult it is. The relationship with the industry produces many obligations. It is a challenge in every project to find a balance.

Hombroich was an important example to show that it is possible, even in Germany, to realize that kind of architecture.
Yes, there was a great freedom in every respect. To see buildings, like the existing ones in Hombroich, in the middle of a fantastic garden, filled with fantastic art, is very lucky. To open the door of such buildings and not to see the usual cameras, air-conditioning, etc. is a great pleasure.

It is interesting that, in Hombroich, an artist has planned the first buildings; maybe this was the only chance to escape the stifling rules and standards.
An architect is also seen as a technician, but here the artist was allowed much more freedom.

I also had an interview with Frei Otto, who has a different approach to architecture, maybe more technical. I asked him, how important form and beauty are to him.
I don't believe that, for example, an engineer cannot work on a spatial concept, but only on the properties of materials, while on the other side the architect cannot work on the properties of materials but instead on the aesthetics. It is this spirit, to separate everything, to fragmentize, that I don't like. When an architect wants to paint or to create sculptures, like in my case, people often say, he has nothing to do with that. I don't believe that. Architecture has to do with many

Es ist interessant, dass in Hombroich die ersten Gebäude von einem Künstler entworfen wurden, vielleicht war das die einzige Möglichkeit, den erdrückenden Vorschriften und Normen zu entkommen.

Ein Architekt wird auch als Techniker gesehen, einem Künstler war es erlaubt, hier war man sicher toleranter.

Ich habe auch ein Interview mit Frei Otto gemacht, der einen anderen Zugang zur Architektur hat, vielleicht einen technischeren. Ich habe ihn gefragt, welche Rolle die Form und die Schönheit für ihn spielen.

Ja, aber er ist keiner, der alles von Spezialisten planen lässt. Es ist nicht so, dass z.B. ein Ingenieur nicht auch an einem Raumkonzept arbeiten könnte, sondern nur an der Belastbarkeit von Materialien, und auf der anderen Seite wäre da der Architekt, der nicht an der Belastbarkeit von Materialien arbeiten könnte, aber der mit der Ästhetik zu tun hat. Es ist dieser Geist, alles aufzuteilen, alles zu fragmentieren, den ich nicht mag. Wenn ein Architekt z.B. malen oder Skulpturen schaffen will, wie in meinem Fall, heißt es oft, er habe damit nichts zu tun, das glaube ich nicht. Architektur hat mit vielem zu tun, mit Musik, mit Kino, mit Tanz, mit Malerei, weil diese Dinge auch alle mit Raum zu tun haben. Es gibt diese unglückliche Tendenz, das Wissen zu fragmentieren,

Ich stimme zu, dass dieses Fragmentieren ein Problem ist, ein Denken in Teilen und nicht ein organisches Denken.

Diese Teilung in Ingenieur des Tragwerks, Ingenieur für Akustik usw. ist unglücklich. Es ist nicht möglich, Spezialist in allem zu sein und alles zu wissen, die Lösung ist es, im Team zusammenzuarbeiten. Für einen Architekten ist das entscheidend.

Letzte Frage: Was können Sie jungen Architekten raten?

Viel und ambitioniert zu arbeiten und viel im Team zu arbeiten.

things, such as music, cinema, dance and painting, because all these things deal with space. There is this unfortunate tendency to fragmentize knowledge.

I agree that this fragmentation is a problem, thinking in parts and not an organic thinking.

This division in structural engineer, engineer for acoustics, etc., is unsuitable. It is not possible to be a specialist in everything; the solution is to work together in a team, but really together. For an architect it is essential.

Last question, what is your advice to young architects?

To work ambitiously and a lot, and to work in a team.

Sporthotel und Hochleistungszentrum
Panticosa, Huesca, Spanien (2001–)

Sports Hotel and High Performance Centre
Panticosa, Huesca, Spain (2001–)

Das Grundstück für das Sporthotel im Kurort Panticosa hat eine Fläche von 3.366 m². Es liegt im Nordwesten des Kurorts, gegenüber der Ortseinfahrt. Das Raumprogramm umfasst ein Hotel für Sportler, einschließlich eines Thermalbads und Sporteinrichtungen. Die Nutzung ist über drei Geschossflächen verteilt: einer Eingangsebene mit Empfang, Restaurant, Bibliothek, Läden und einer großen Halle; einem Obergeschoss für alle Schlafzimmer; einem Untergeschoss mit Umkleideräumen und Sportstudio. Die Ebene für die Sporteinrichtungen ist mittels Plattformen organisiert, die alle durch eine Rampenpromenade verbunden sind, welche zum Schwimmbecken führt. Diese Einrichtungen werden auf dem Dach über Solarium und Außenschwimmbecken weitergeführt. In die Pracht des gegebenen Ensembles fügt sich das Gebäude in gelungener Weise ein und wird zu einem verbindenden Element zwischen dem Berg und den eher städtischen Elementen des Kurorts. Das Gebäude verschwindet größtenteils im Erdboden, um so die Wirkung des Hotels im oberen Bereich des Grundstücks zu minimieren, so dass es städtischer wird und sich mit dem Eingangsbereich in der Nähe des Hotel Continental verbindet. Aufgrund der topographischen Eigenschaften ist das Sporthotel von den Zufahrten entlang des Bergs, von den Hotels und von den anderen Einrichtungen im Sportbereich aus sichtbar. Aus allen diesen Blickrichtungen wird das Dach zu einem klar erkennbaren Element. Die Landschaftsgestaltung dieser Ebene ist daher von größter Bedeutung. Man erreicht dieses Gebäude nach Durchquerung einer Baumgruppe und dem Gang entlang einer Mauer, welche die Besucher zum Empfangsbereich führt. An diesem Punkt beginnt eine Raumsequenz, die zum Dach führt. Von hier aus bietet sich ein Panoramablick auf die Landschaft. Die Elemente, die die räumliche Organisation des Gebäudes letztlich artikulieren, sind tatsächlich dieser externe Weg sowie jener, der sich innerhalb des Sportstudios fortsetzt.

The site for the Sports Hotel in the spa resort of Panticosa has an area of 3,366 m². It lies to the northwest of the spa, opposite to its entrance. The program is a hotel for athletes, including a spa and sports facilities. The program is distributed over three basic levels: an access level for the reception, restaurant, library, shop and a large hall; an upper level for all of the bedrooms; a basement containing the changing rooms and gymnasium. The level for the sports facilities is organized by means of platforms, all of which are connected by a promenade of ramps, leading to the indoor swimming pool. These facilities continue to the roof level by way of the solarium and the outdoor swimming pool. Given the magnificence of the location, the building engages with it in a good willed manner, becoming a connecting element between the mountain and the more urban elements of the spa town. The building largely disappears into the ground, so as to minimize the hotel's impact at the upper level of the site, thus becoming more urban and engaged with its access area, close to the Hotel Continental. Given the topographic characteristics, the Sports Hotel is apparent from the approaches along the mountain, from the hotels, and from other facilities in the spa. From all these points, its roof level becomes a clearly visible element. The landscaping of this level is therefore of great importance. One arrives at the complex by traversing a group of trees and moving along a wall which guides the visitor to the reception area. At that point, a sequence begins that leads one to the roof. From there, a panoramic view of the landscape is obtained. The elements articulating the spatial organization of the building are, in fact, this external route and also the one which takes place within the sports area.

Beziehung zum Gelände / Relation to site ▸

Blick von Westen / View from west

Dach / Roof

72 Sportzentrum Panticosa

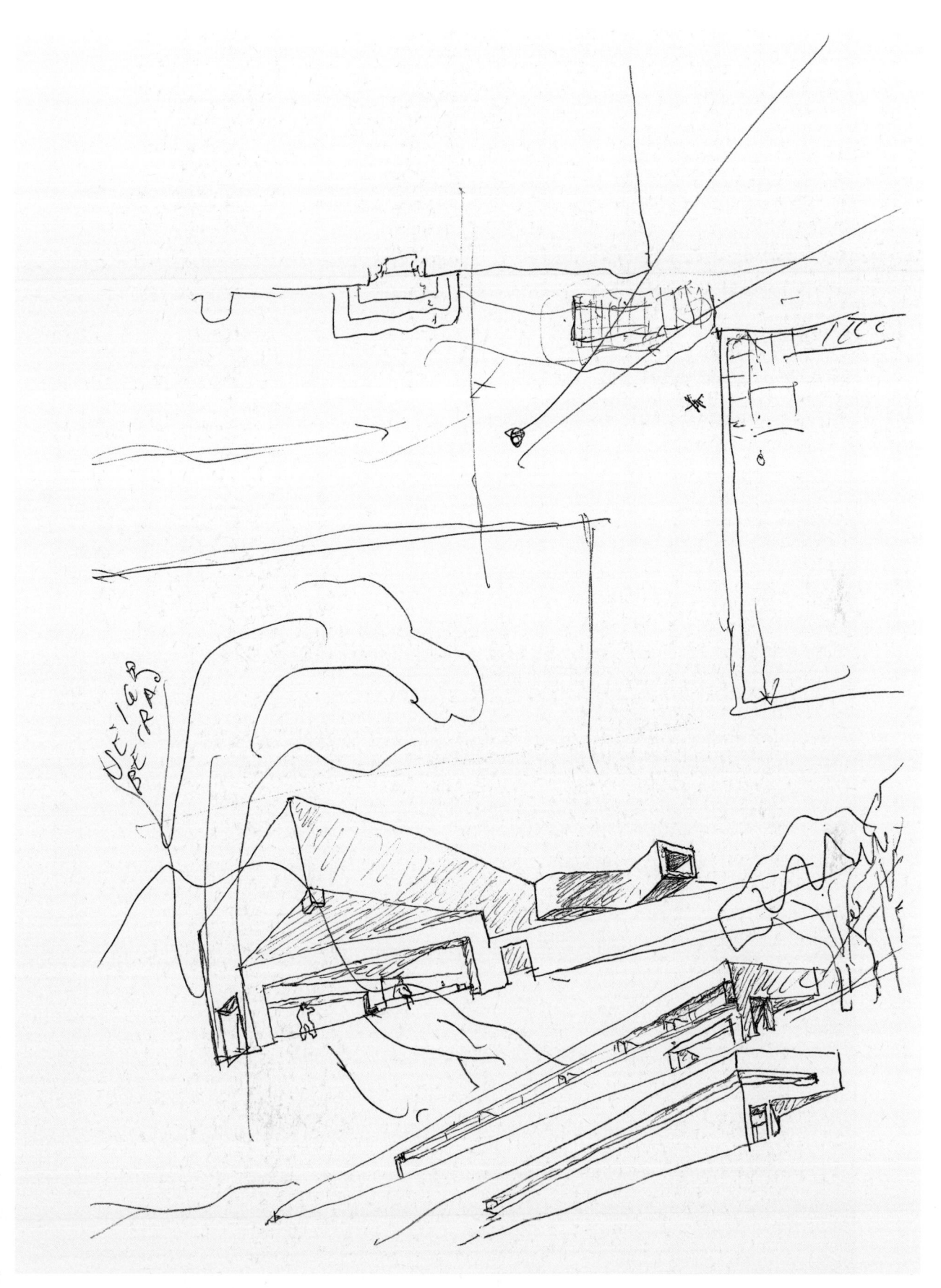

Skizze Eingang / Entrance sketch

Sports center Panticosa

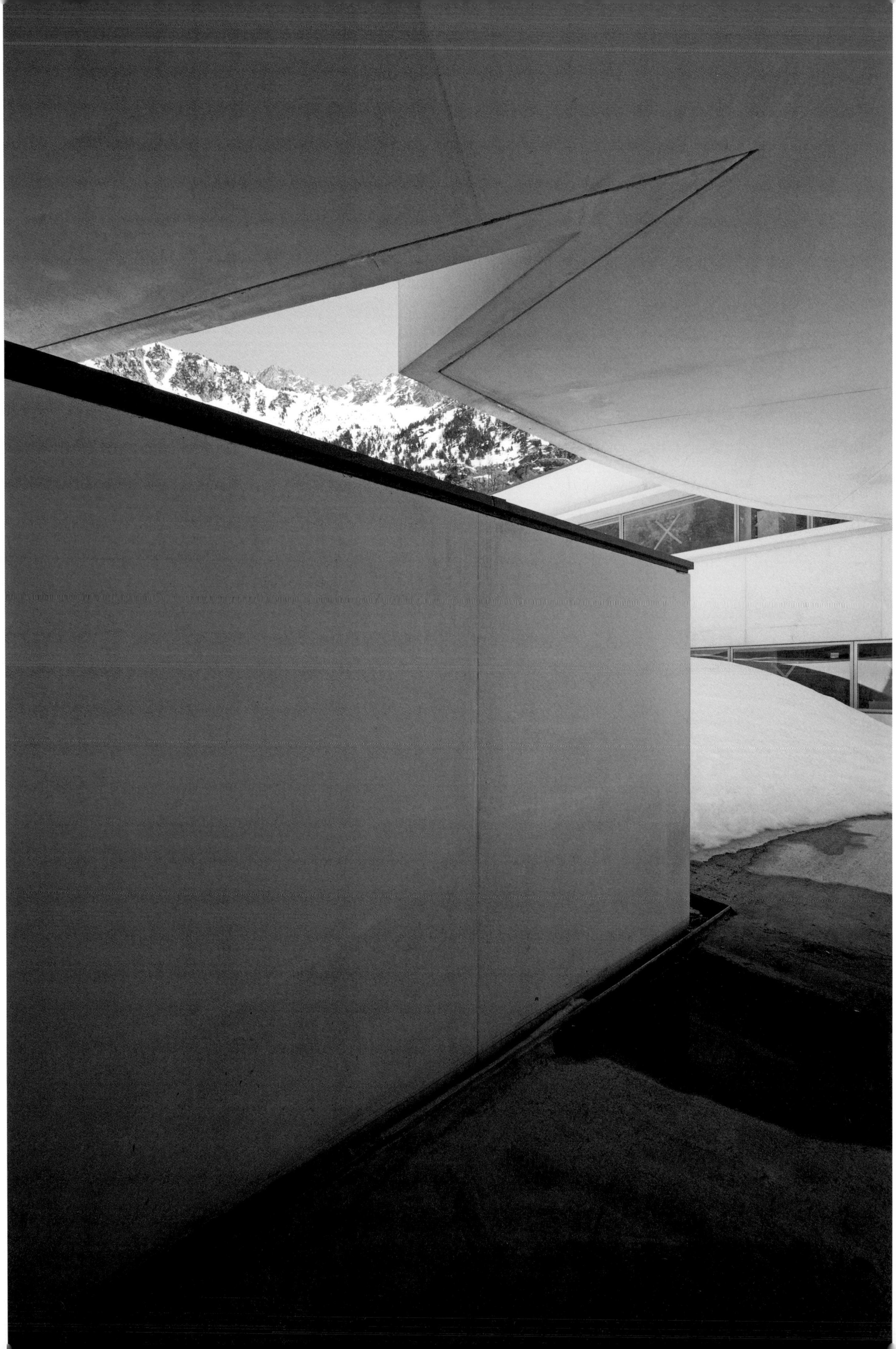

Brücke / Bridge

Studien / Studies

◂ *Eingang / Entrance*

Sports center Panticosa 75

Innenraumskizzen mit Höhen / Interior studies with heights

Empfang / Reception

76   Sportzentrum Panticosa

Sporthalle / Sports Hall

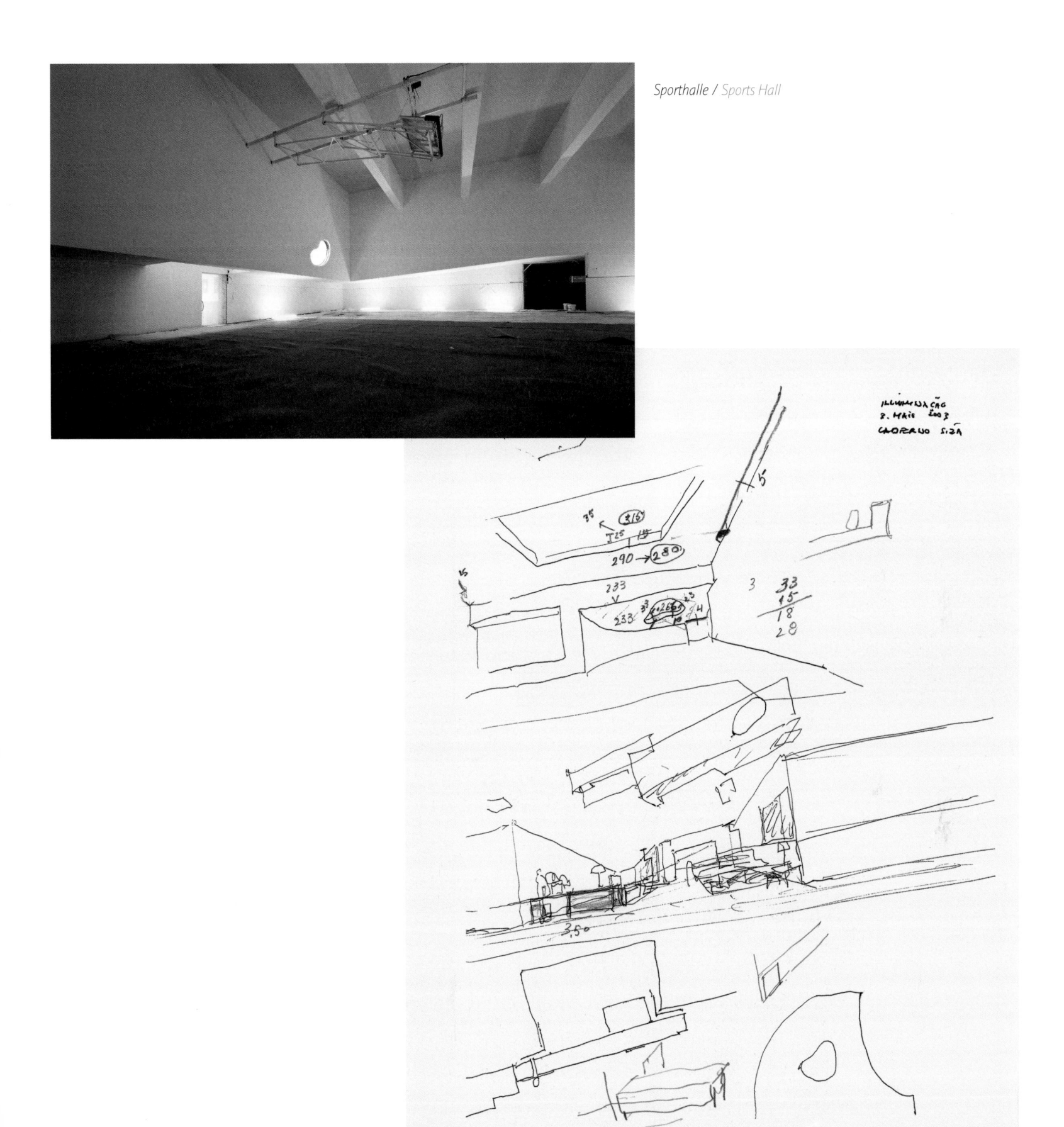

Innenraumskizzen / Interior sketches

Sports center Panticosa

Gesamtmodell / Complete model

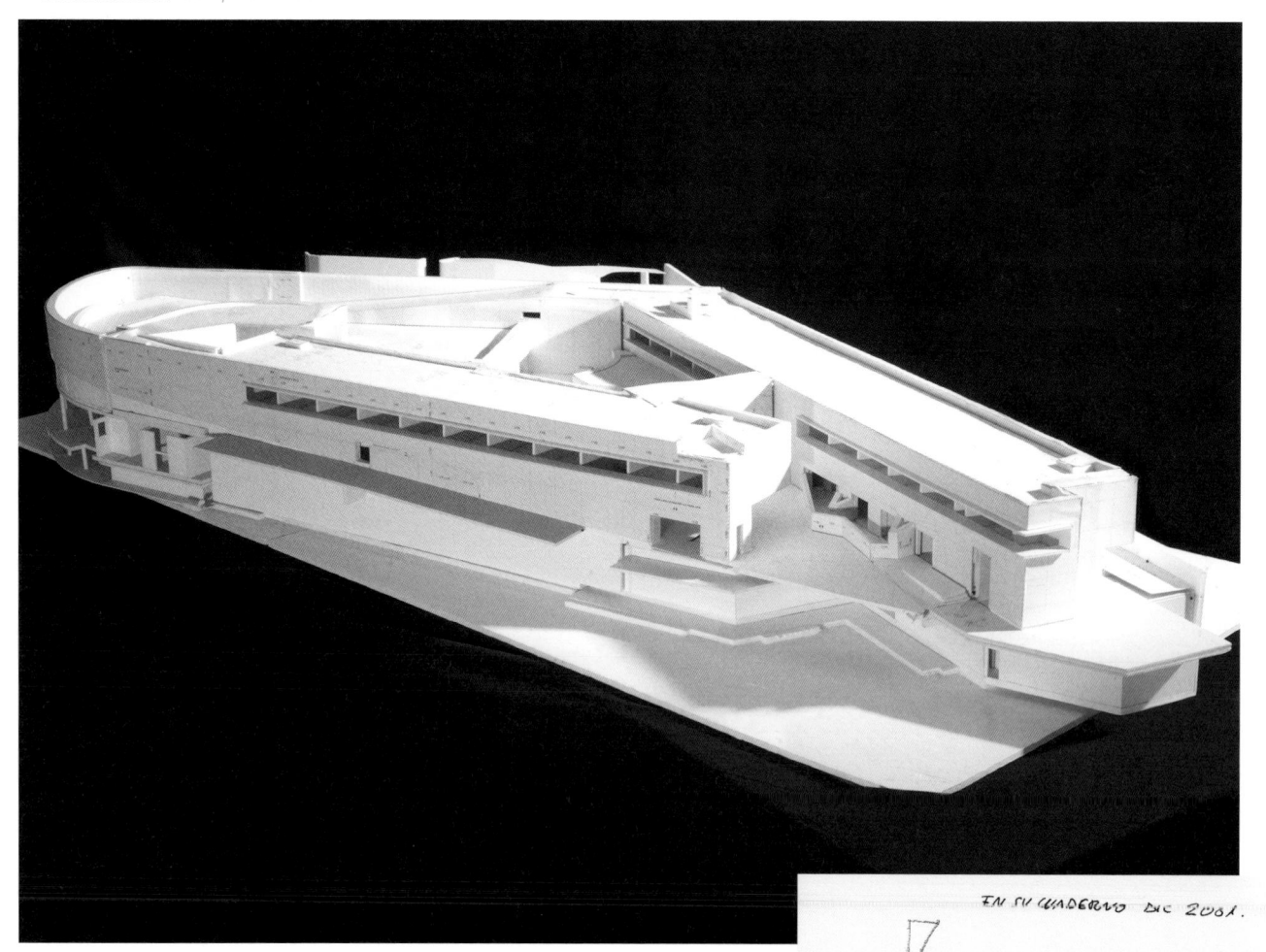

Volumenstudie / Volume studies

78   Sportzentrum Panticosa

Grundriss Erdgeschoss / Ground floor plan

1	Technischer Bereich
2	Technischer Tank
3	Thermalwassertank
4	Sporthalle
5	Hydrogymnastik-Pool
6	Ruheraum
7	Lager
8	Bibliothek
9	Halle
10	Eingang
11	Verwaltung
12	WC
13	Restaurant
14	Küche
15	Technischer Bereich
16	Lager

1	Technical Area
2	Technical Tank
3	Thermal Water Tank
4	Sports Hall
5	Hydrogymnastic Pool
6	Relaxing Area
7	Store
8	Library
9	Hall
10	Reception
11	Administration
12	WC
13	Restaurant
14	Kitchen
15	Technical Room
16	Storage

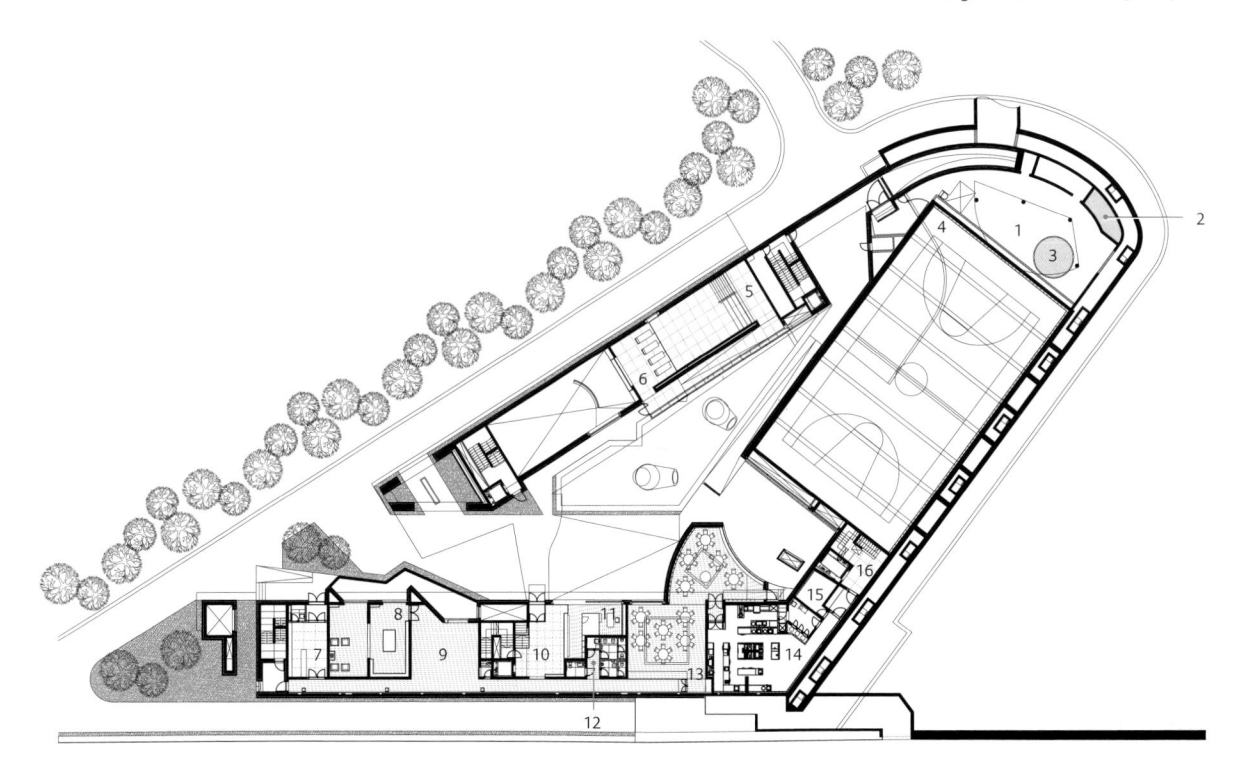

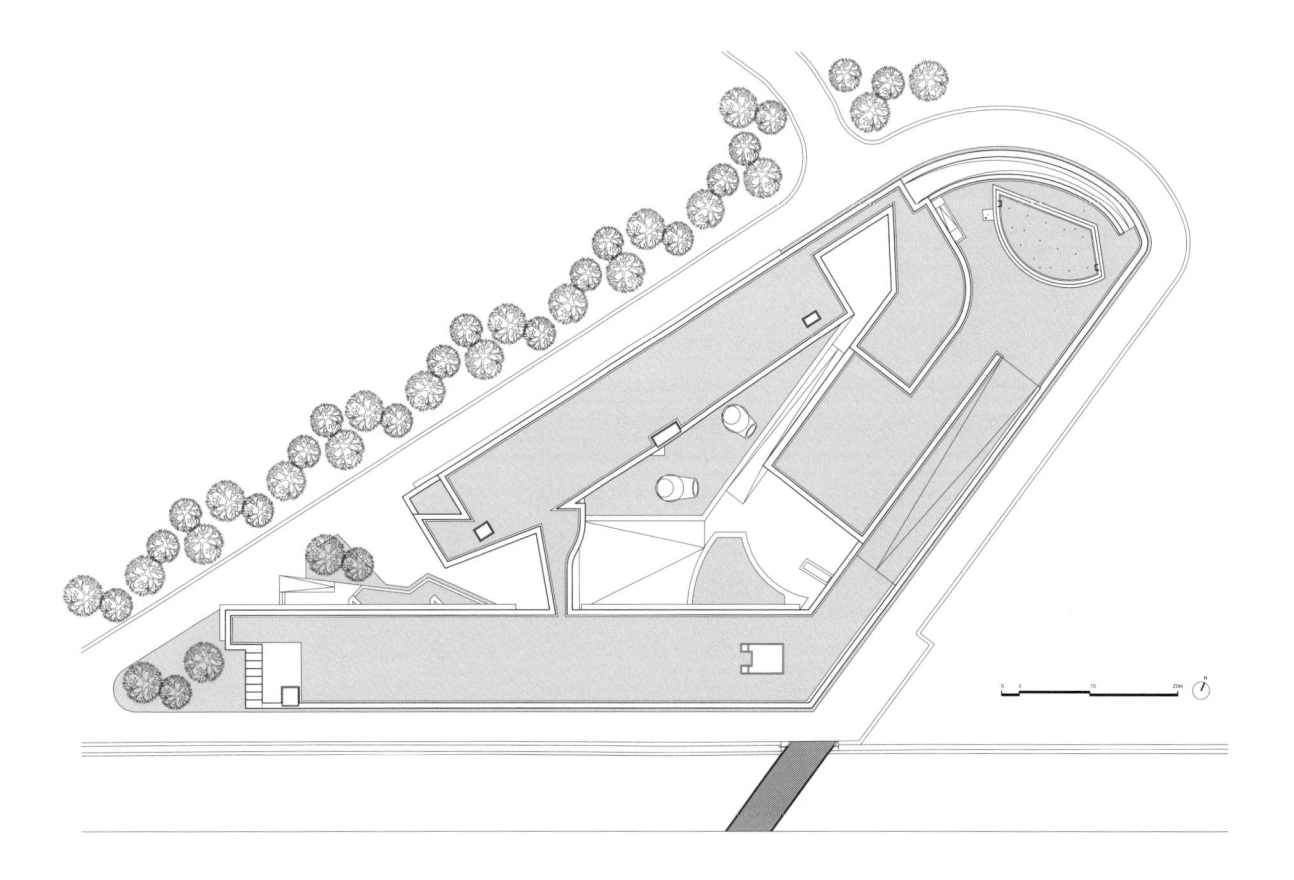

Dachplan / Roof plan

Sports center Panticosa

Serralves Museum für zeitgenössische Kunst
Porto, Portugal (1991–1999)

Serralves Museum of Contemporary Art
Oporto, Portugal (1991–1999)

Einmal mehr wurde ich gebeten, ein Museum in einen bestehenden Park einzufügen — ein exquisiter Park, welcher eine Folge wohldefinierter Räume beinhaltet: einen klassischen Park, einen romantischen Park mit einem See, einen landwirtschaftlichen Bereich und einen Bereich, der einmal ein Obstgarten war, der dann an den Garten angeschlossen wurde, aber ursprünglich nicht Teil der Gesamtprojekts war. Ich entschied mich, das Gebäude in den ehemaligen Obstgarten zu legen, so dass es zu einem Element werden würde, welches einen intensiveren Besucherverkehr innerhalb der Wege durch den Park hervorrufen würde. Ein Fußweg beginnt im landwirtschaftlichen Bereich und kehrt zum Ausgangspunkt am Museum zurück, parallel entlang des Hauses verlaufend. Von hier aus entwickelt ein weiterer Weg eine Beziehung zum Haus. Es ist beabsichtigt, die komplexe Raumreihenfolge zu vervollständigen, um somit einen ganzheitlichen Park zu schaffen.   Das Raumprogramm wurde während der Entwurfsphase verändert, es wechselten auch die Regierungen. Drei vorläufige Studien wurden entworfen, bevor das endgültige Raumprogramm festgelegt wurde. Jedes dieser Raumprogramme war von der Einfügung des Museums in den Park wie auch von der offensichtlichen Sorge in Bezug auf dessen Auswirkung auf den Park und die umliegenden Straßen geprägt. Es war daher erforderlich, ein großformatiges Gebäude mit einer beträchtlichen Gesamtfläche zu errichten, welches keinen nennenswerten Effekt auf das Umfeld (ein Wohnviertel mit zweistöckigen Wohnhäusern) haben und in Einklang mit dem kostbaren Park stehen oder ihn ergänzen sollte. Die Notwendigkeit, den Effekt des Gebäudes zu verringern, war einer der Gründe, weshalb es so steil angelegt ist (dem Lauf des Grundstücks folgend) und weshalb sich die Lagerflächen entweder unterirdisch oder halbunterirdisch befinden und somit die Zulieferung am oberen Ende ermöglichen, am niedrigsten Punkt des Geländes.   In einer gewissen Weise ist das Gebäude auch aufgebrochen: Der Körper des Hörsaals, der Körper des Museums, einschließlich der Gemeinschafts- und Ausstellungsflächen, sind in einen »U«-Baukörper gefasst, welcher somit den Park zu einem Bestandteil des Museums werden lässt und die Auswirkung des Museums auf die Umgebung minimiert. Das Konzept ähnelt jenem für das Museum in Santiago de Compostela und umfasst eine Folge von unterschiedlich bemaßten Räumen auf zwei Ebenen.

Once again I was asked to insert a museum within an existing park — an exquisite park incorporating a succession of well-defined spaces: a classical park, a romantic park with a lake, an agricultural area, and a space which had been an orchard and which was later annexed to the garden but which did not form part of the initial project. I chose to locate the museum in the former orchard, so that it would constitute an element that would foster greater movement within the set of paths through the park. One path begins at the agricultural area and then returns to the museum's location, running laterally in relation to the House. From this space another path establishes a relationship with the House. The intention is to complete the complex succession of spaces, thus constituting a single park.   The programme underwent changes during the design period and there were also changes of government. Three preliminary studies were drawn up before the final programme was fixed. All these programmes were guided by the museum's insertion within the park, together with the obvious concern raised in relation to the impact on the park and the surrounding streets. It was therefore necessary to build a large-scale building, with a significant interior area, that would not have a major impact on the surroundings (a residential quarter with two-storey buildings) and which would be in harmony with, or complement the high-quality park. This need to reduce the impact of the building was one of the reasons why it is steeply sloped (following the lie of the land) and why the storage areas are located either underground or partially submerged, thus enabling access for loading and unloading at the upper end, at the lowest level of the terrain.   To a certain extent, the building is also fragmented: the body of the auditorium, and the body of the museum, including the social and exhibition areas, are developed in a U-shaped configuration, enabling the park to be part of the museum's volume, thus minimizing its environmental impact. The concept is similar to that of Santiago de Compostela, and consists of a succession of rooms of different dimensions on two levels.

expandido
2005
düsseldsch

Skizze mit Park / Sketch with park

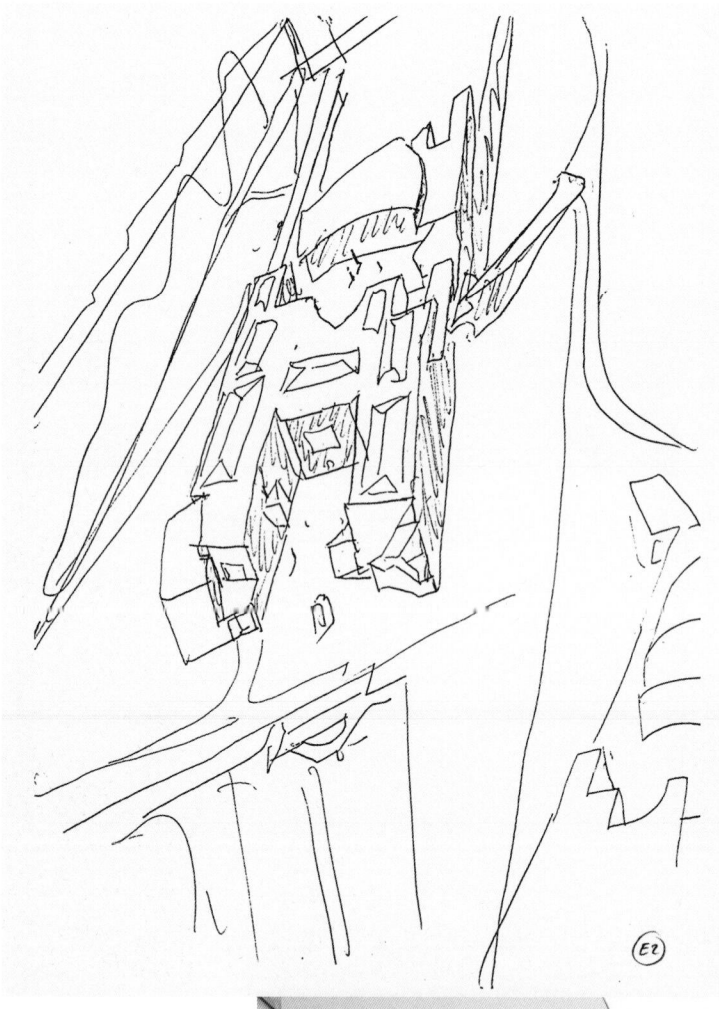

Teilmodell / Partial model

Südlicher Innenhof / South courtyard

82   Museum Serralves

Vorstudien / Prestudies

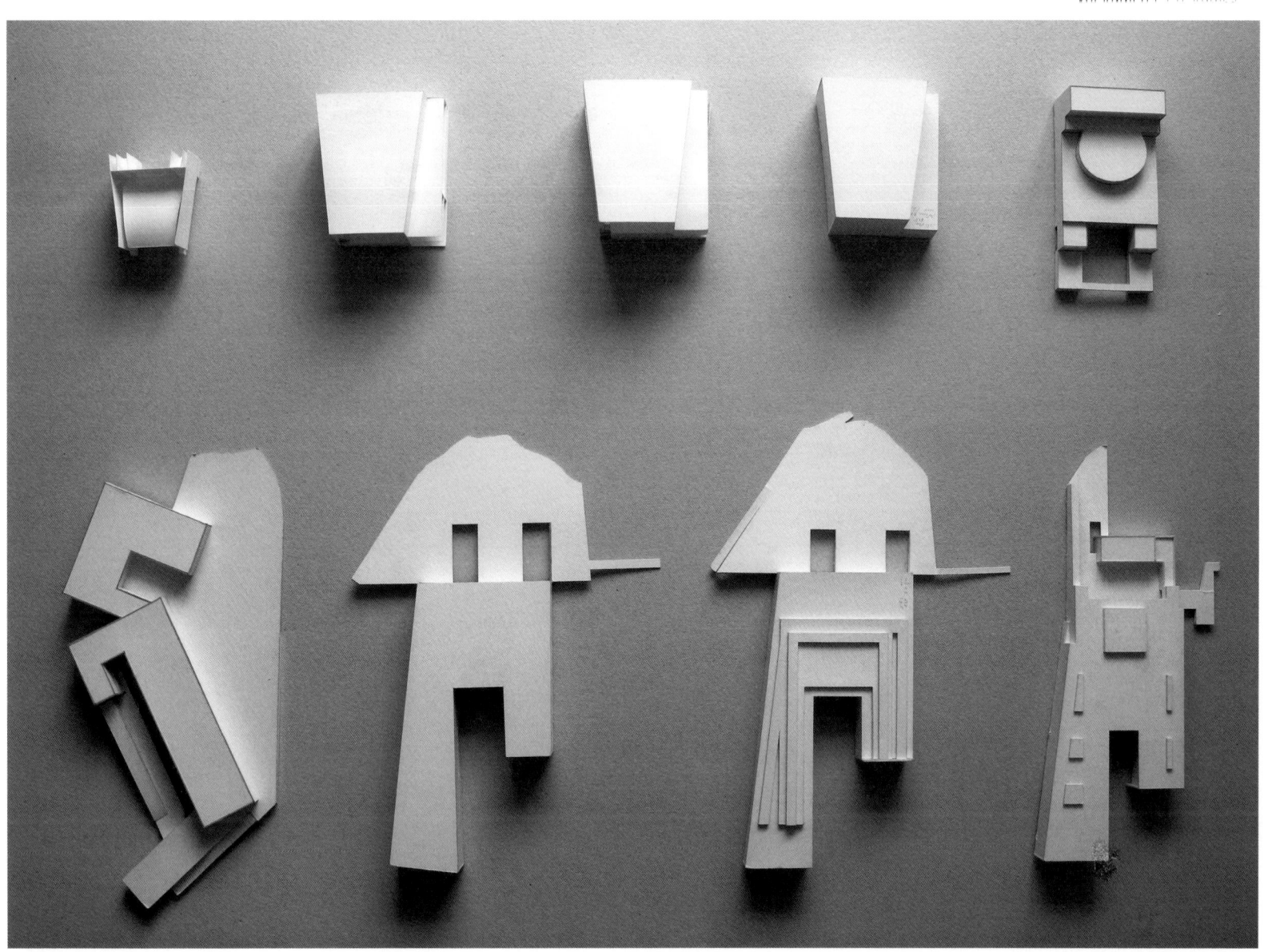

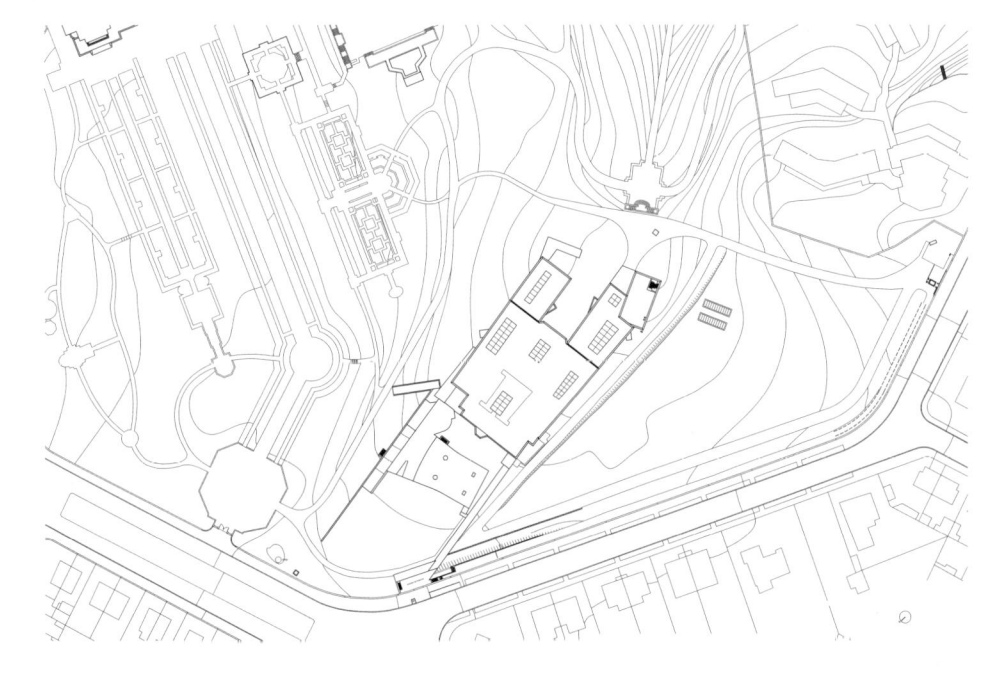

Lageplan / Site plan

Museum Serralves

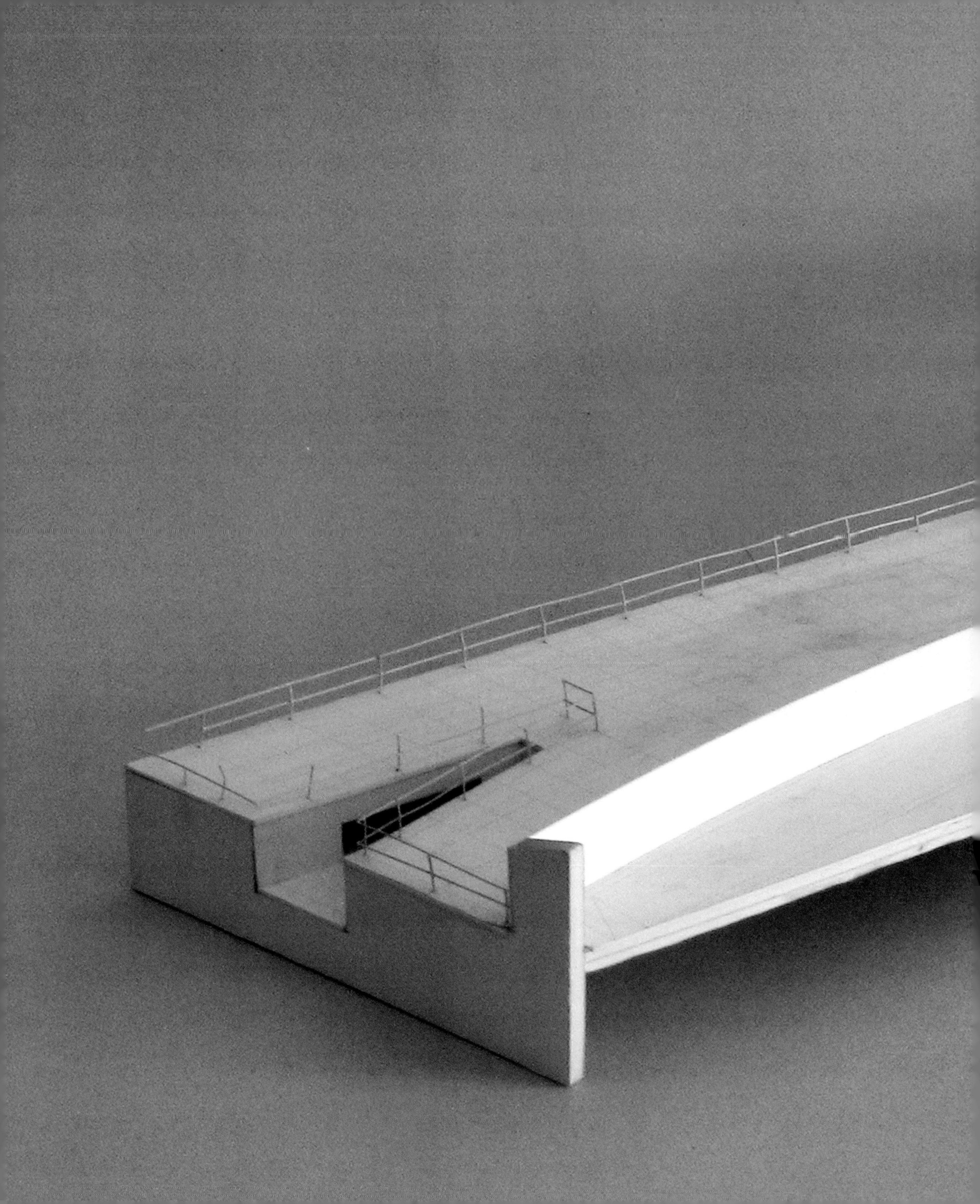

Modell Terrasse / Model of terrace

#	German	#	German	#	English
1	Arbeitsraum / Ausstellung	30	Überdachte Rampe	14	Circulation
2	Balkon	31	Vorplatz	15	Light Cannon
3	Ausstellungsraum 1	32	Rampe	16	Antechamber
4	Ausstellungsraum 2	33	Eingang Hof	17	Storage
5	Ausstellungsraum 3	34	Zufahrtsrampe Hof	18	Central Hall
6	Ausstellungsraum 4	35	Ticketschalter	19	Foyer Dressing Room
7	Ausstellungsraum 5	36	Foyer Auditorium	20	Foyer Entrance
8	Ausstellungsraum 6	37	Garderobe Auditorium	21	Access Store
9	Ausstellungsraum 7	38	Technischer Bereich	22	Access Foyer
10	Ausstellungsraum 8	39	Technische Service	23	Bookshop
11	Ausstellungsraum 9	40	Licht-Box	24	Extra Store
12	Ausstellungsraum 10	41	Übersetzungs-Box	25	Information Desk
13	Ausstellungsraum 11	42	WC	26	Cloakroom
14	Erschließung			27	Storage
15	Lichtkanone			28	Covered Court
16	Vorzimmer			29	Exterior Court
17	Lager	1	Working Room / Exhibition	30	Covered Ramp
18	Zentrale Halle	2	Balcony	31	Entrance Court
19	Foyer Garderobe	3	Exhibition Room 1	32	Ramp
20	Foyer Eingang	4	Exhibition Room 2	33	Entrance to Court
21	Zugang Lager	5	Exhibition Room 3	34	Access Ramp to Court
22	Zugang Foyer	6	Exhibition Room 4	35	Box-Office
23	Buchhandlung	7	Exhibition Room 5	36	Auditorium Foyer
24	Zusatzlager	8	Exhibition Room 6	37	Cloakroom of the Auditorium
25	Information	9	Exhibition Room 7	38	Technical Area
26	Garderobe	10	Exhibition Room 8	39	Technical Circulation
27	Lager	11	Exhibition Room 9	40	Light Box
28	Überdachter Hof	12	Exhibition Room 10	41	Translation Box
29	Äußerer Hof	13	Exhibition Room 11	42	WC

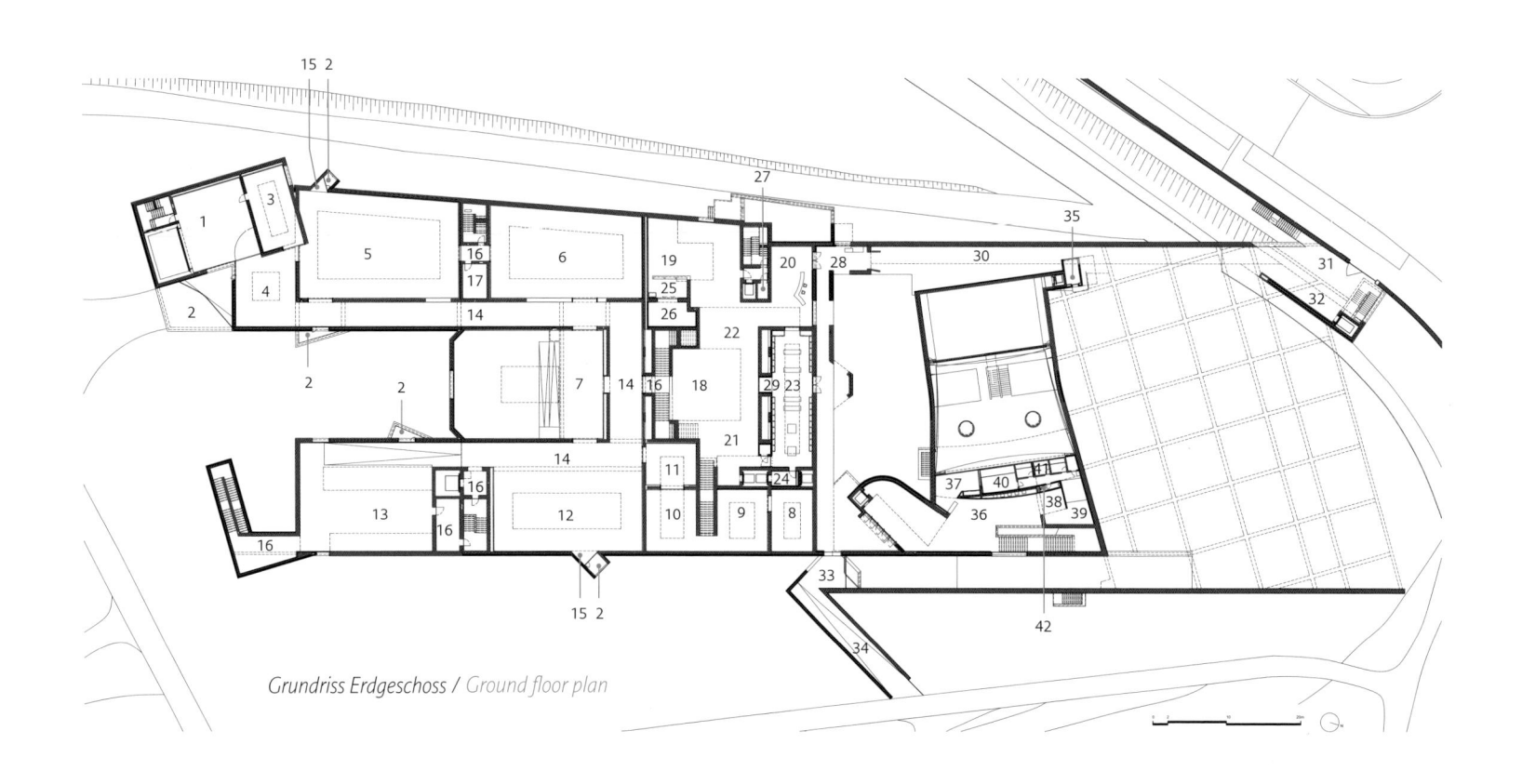

Grundriss Erdgeschoss / Ground floor plan

Ausstellungsräume / Exhibition spaces

Detailskizzen / Detail sketches

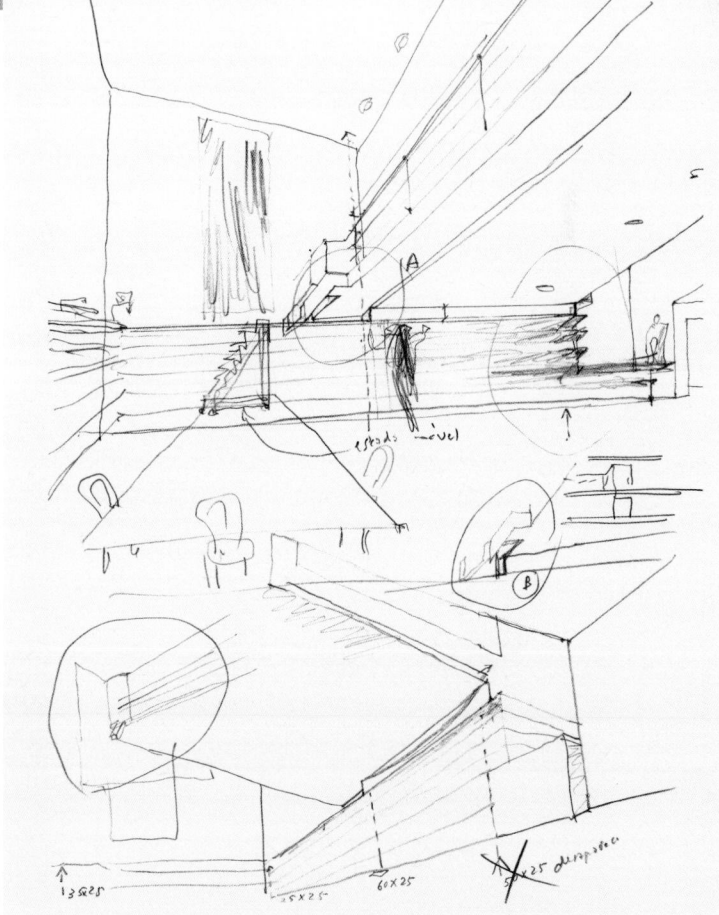

Museum Serralves 87

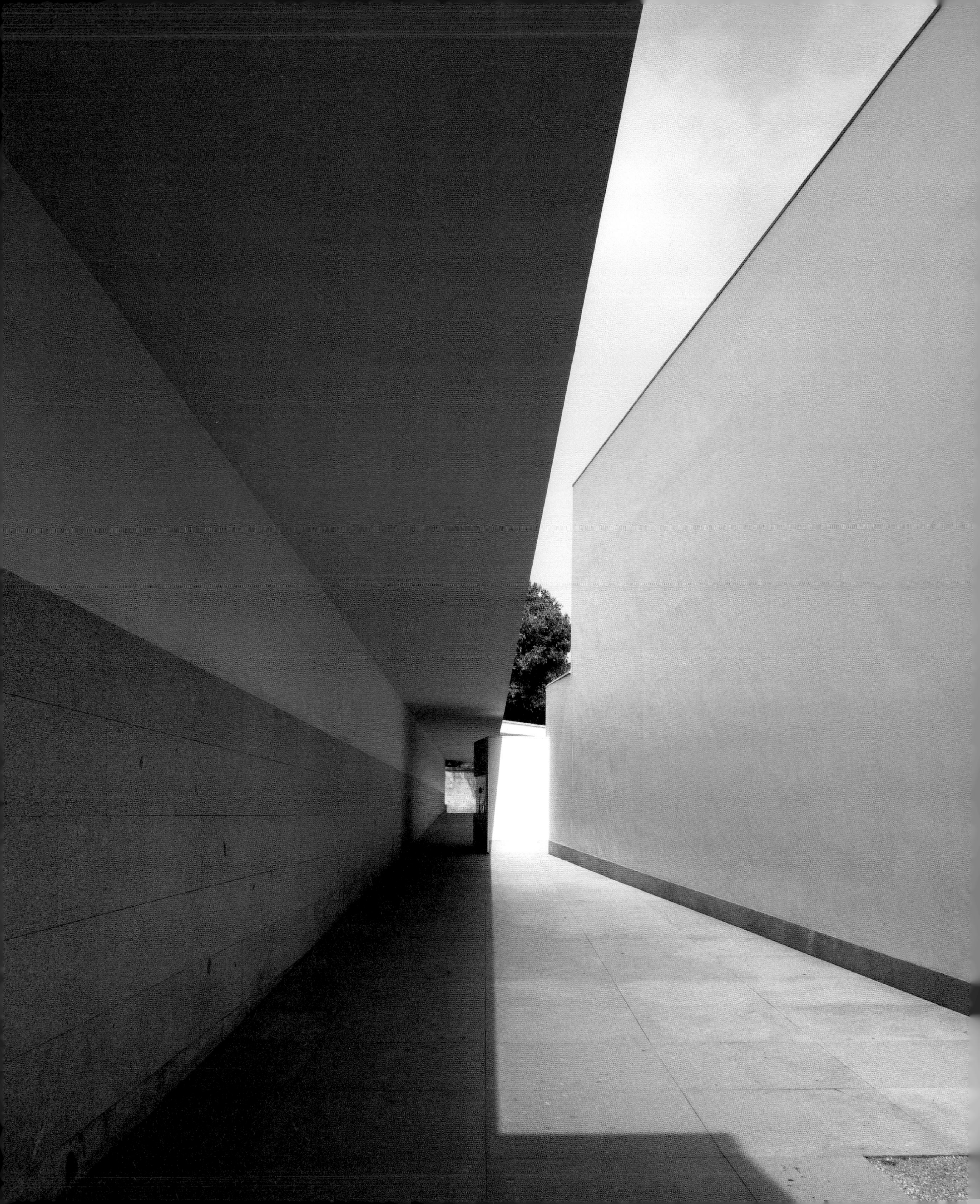

Skizze Eingang / Entrance sketch

Vorhof / Forecourt

Museum mit Park / Museum with Park

◂ *Zugang / Exterior walkway*

Museum Serralves

Anyang Pavillon
Young-Il Park, Südkorea (2005–2006)

Anyang Pavilion
Young-Il Park, South Korea (2005–2006)

Eine kleine Stadt mit 300.000 Einwohnern war die Initiatorin eines Kulturzentrums, welches sich am Eingangsbereich eines natürlichen Parks, mitten in einem schönen Gebirge, befinden sollte. Es wurde ein Multifunktionspavillon als eine Ergänzung hierzu, aber auch als zentraler, für jeden zugänglichen Teil der Gesamtkomposition benötigt ...   Das Raumprogramm war spärlich, es forderte einen Multifunktionsraum, ein kleines Büro, eventuell für die Polizei, und Toiletten für die Parkbesucher sowie für die Benutzer des benachbarten Platzes und für die Restaurantgäste ... Der Ort ist eine Öffnung / ein offener Raum, der im Gebirge geschaffen wird, für einen Platz, der noch hergestellt werden muss.   ... die Form nimmt mit der Auflösung der Aufgabe Gestalt an ...   Die Grundform ist zur Gänze in grauem Beton ausgeführt, er ist so fein, dass er fast weiß ist ... Die Ausführung ist perfekt, trotz des Termindrucks. Der Ort ist wie für diesen Baukörper geschaffen und der Baukörper wächst aus ihm heraus ...   Der Raum ist nicht statisch ... Er ist introvertiert, wenn er so zu sein hat, extrovertiert in seinen Perspektiven, seinen Wegen, in seinen räumlichen Formen und in seinen Materialien.

A small town of 300,000 inhabitants had initiated the development of a cultural centre at the entrance to a natural park, located amidst beautiful mountains. As an addition but central to the composition, a multifunction pavilion, accessible to all, would be required ...   The brief was sparse; it included a multifunctional space, a small office, perhaps for the police, and toilets for the use by people visiting the park and the nearby square and restaurants ...   The location is an opening/open space made in the mountain, a square yet to be created.   ... the form begins to take shape with the resolution of the brief ...   The basic volume is complete in grey concrete so fine it's almost white ... Execution is perfect despite the urgency. The place was made for this volume and the volume grows out of it ...   The space is not static ... It is introverted when it needs to be, extroverted in its perspectives, its routes, in its volumetric form and in the materials.

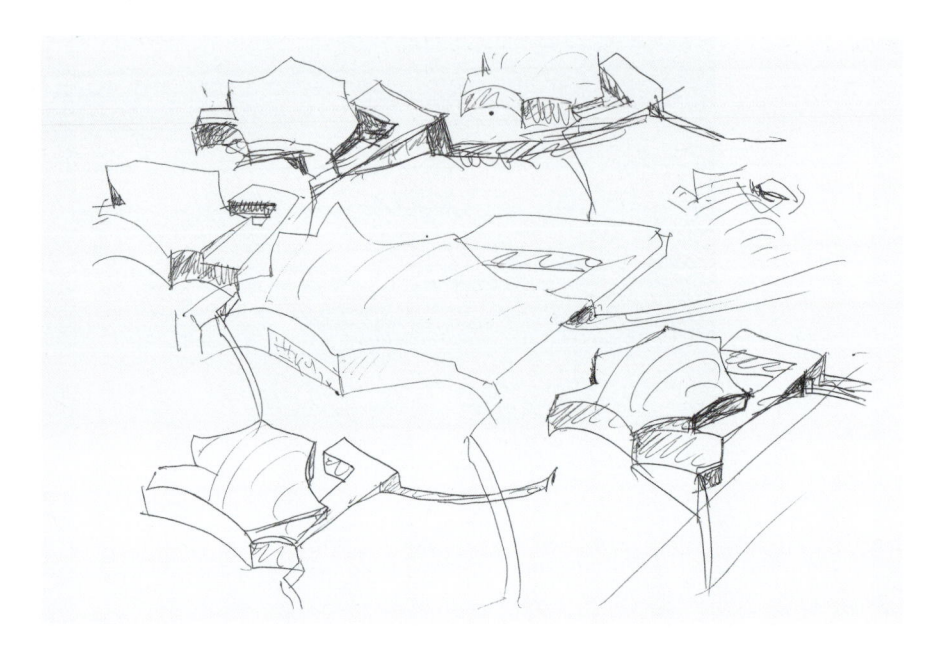

Eingang / Entrance

◂ *Formenstudien / Form studies*

Pavilion Anyang

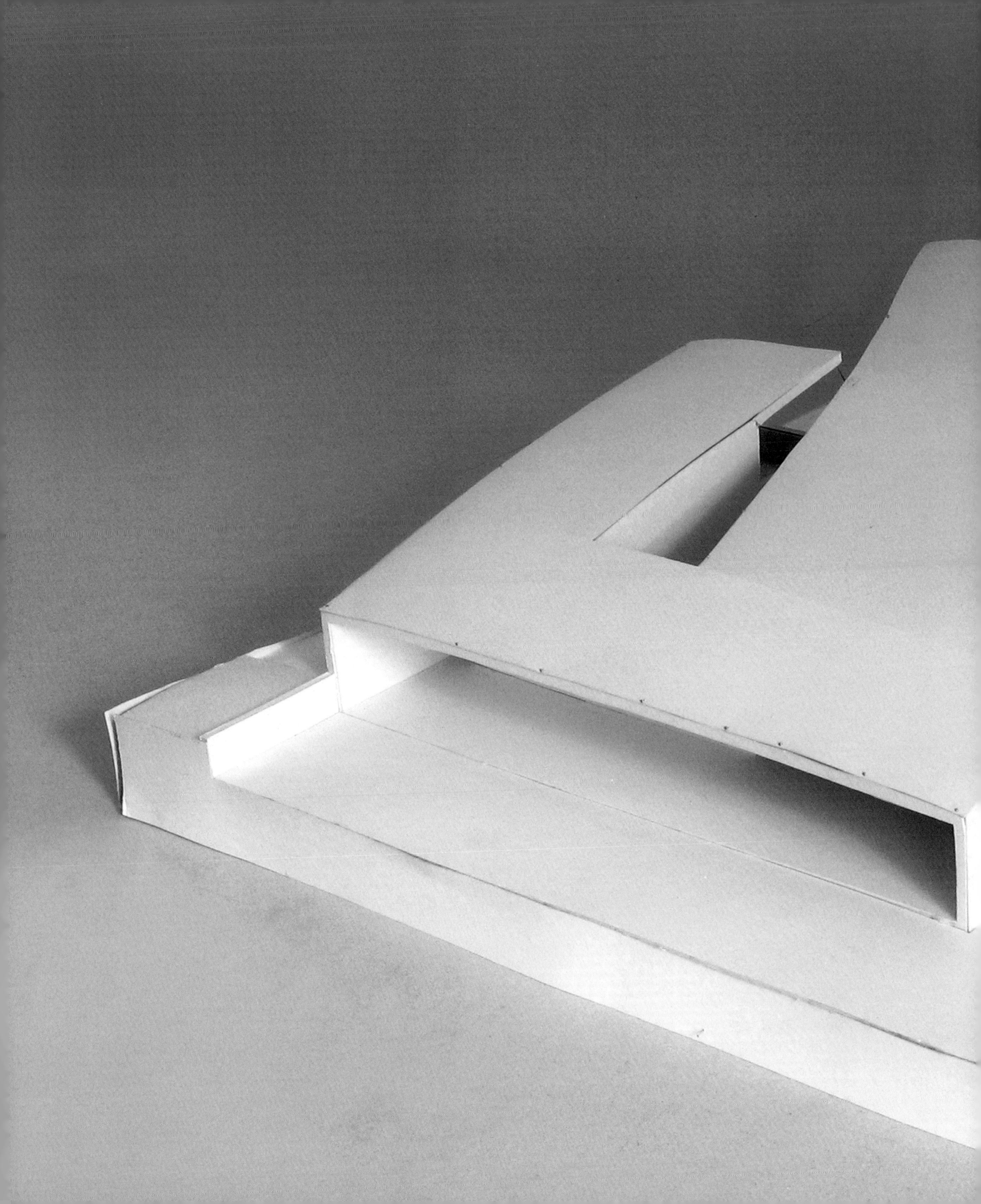

Blick zum Eingang / View to entrance

Südfassade / South facade

Detailskizzen / Detail sketches

94　Pavillon Anyang

Lageplan / *Site plan*

Modell / *Model*

Pavilion Anyang

Balkon zum Hauptraum / Balcony to main space

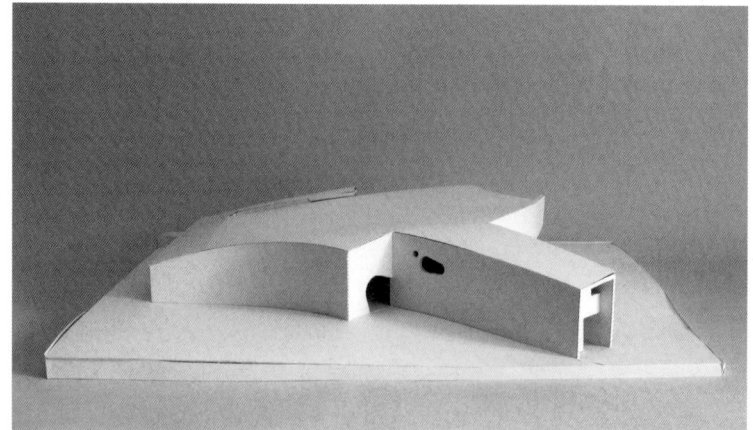

1 Öffentlicher Eingang
2 Ausstellungshalle
3 Nebeneingang
4 Treppe
5 Raum
6 WC
7 Archiv
8 Sicherheitsraum
9 Eingang
10 Service Eingang
11 WC

1 Public Entrance
2 Exhibition Hall
3 Secondary Entrance
4 Stairs
5 Room
6 WC
7 Archive
8 Security-Room
9 Entrance
10 Service Entrance
11 WC

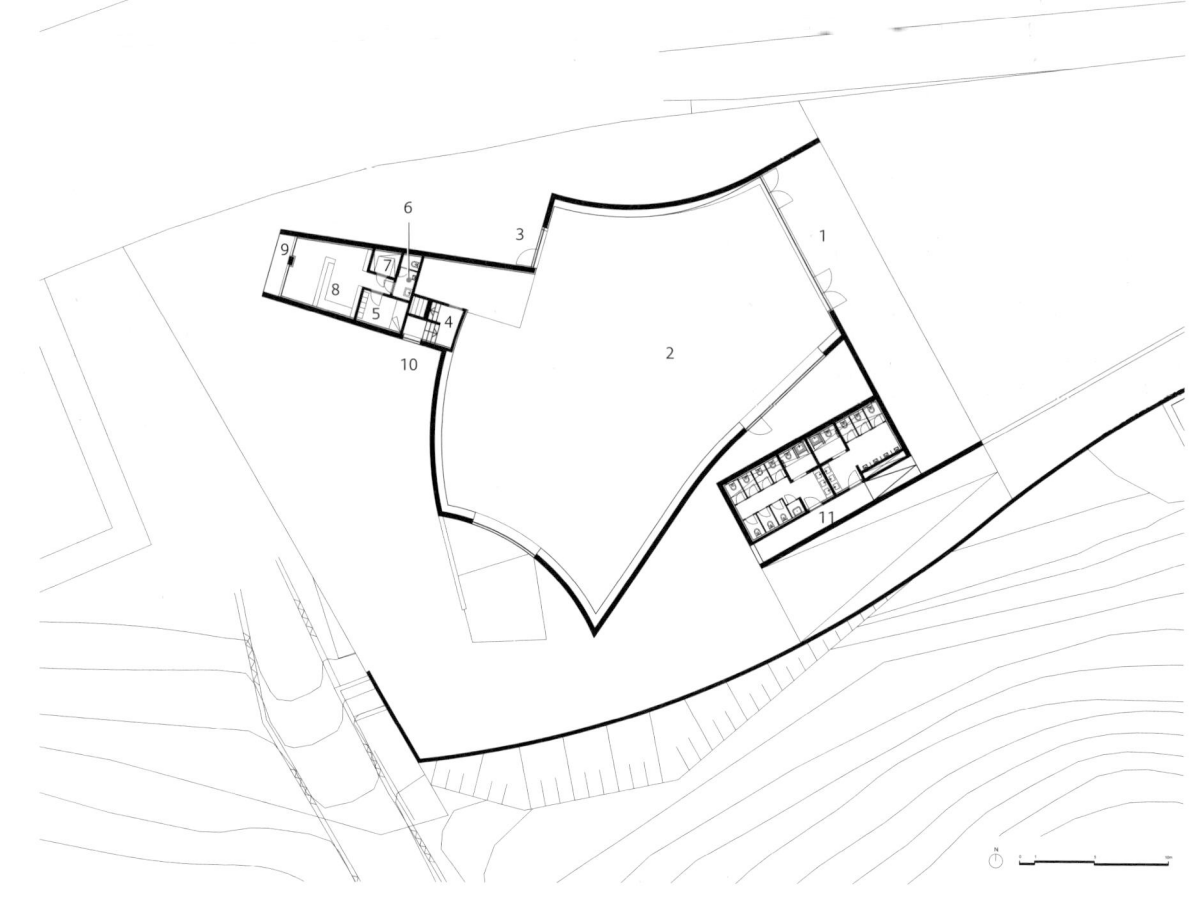

Grundriss Erdgeschoss / Ground floor plan

Hauptraum / Main space

Mimesis Museum
Paju Book City, Südkorea (2006–2009) **Mit Carlos Castanheira und Jun Sung Kim**

Mimesis Museum
Paju Book City, South Korea (2006–2009) **With Carlos Castanheira and Jun Sung Kim**

Dieses Museum wurde für eine zeitgenössische Kunstsammlung entworfen. Es befindet sich in einem wachsenden Viertel der Bücherstadt Paju, Südkorea. Das vorgesehene Programm ist über einen Keller, zwei Geschosse und ein Zwischengeschoss verteilt. Im Keller sind das Archiv und die Technik untergebracht. Empfang, Wechselausstellungshalle und das Café befinden sich im Erdgeschoss. Die Zwischenebene nimmt die Verwaltung und den Museumladen auf. Ein weiterer Ausstellungsraum befindet sich im Obergeschoss. Der Baukörper ist durch gekurvte Flächen aus weißem Beton definiert, die einen Hof umschließen und sich an einem Ende des Gebäudes nach außen öffnen. Die Ausstellungsräume sind über die größte Fläche indirekt und zenital durch natürliches und künstliches Licht beleuchtet.

This museum has been designed for a specific contemporary art collection. It is located in a growth area of Paju Book City, South Korea.

The proposed program is distributed across a basement, a mezzanine, and two floors. The basement contains an archive and technical equipment. The reception, temporary exhibition space and cafeteria are located at ground level. The mezzanine holds the administration and a museum shop. There is another exhibition space on the top floor. The building's configuration is defined by curved surfaces of white concrete which envelop a yard, and which open at one end of the building. The exhibition areas are lit via the largest surface indirectly from above by natural and artificial means.

Eingang / Entrance

Erste Skizze / Initial sketch

Eingangshof / Entrance courtyard

Eingang / Entrance

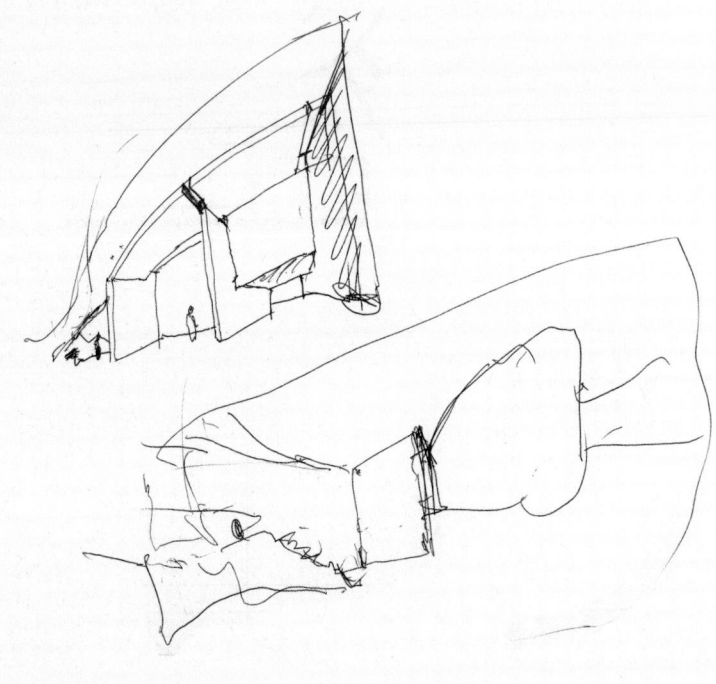

Foyer Skizze / Foyer sketch

100 **Museum Mimesis**

Blick auf Eingang / View towards entrance

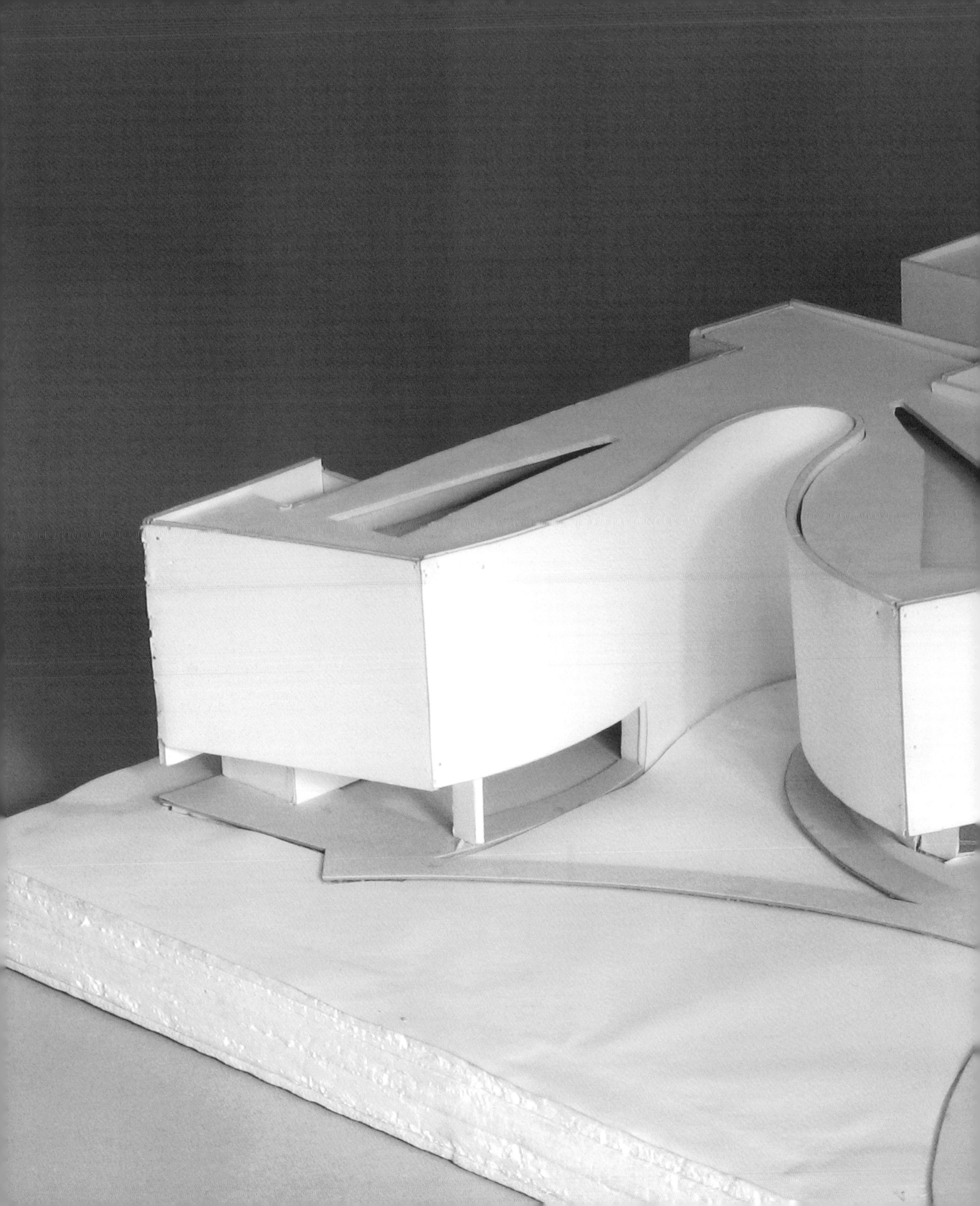

Modell / Modul

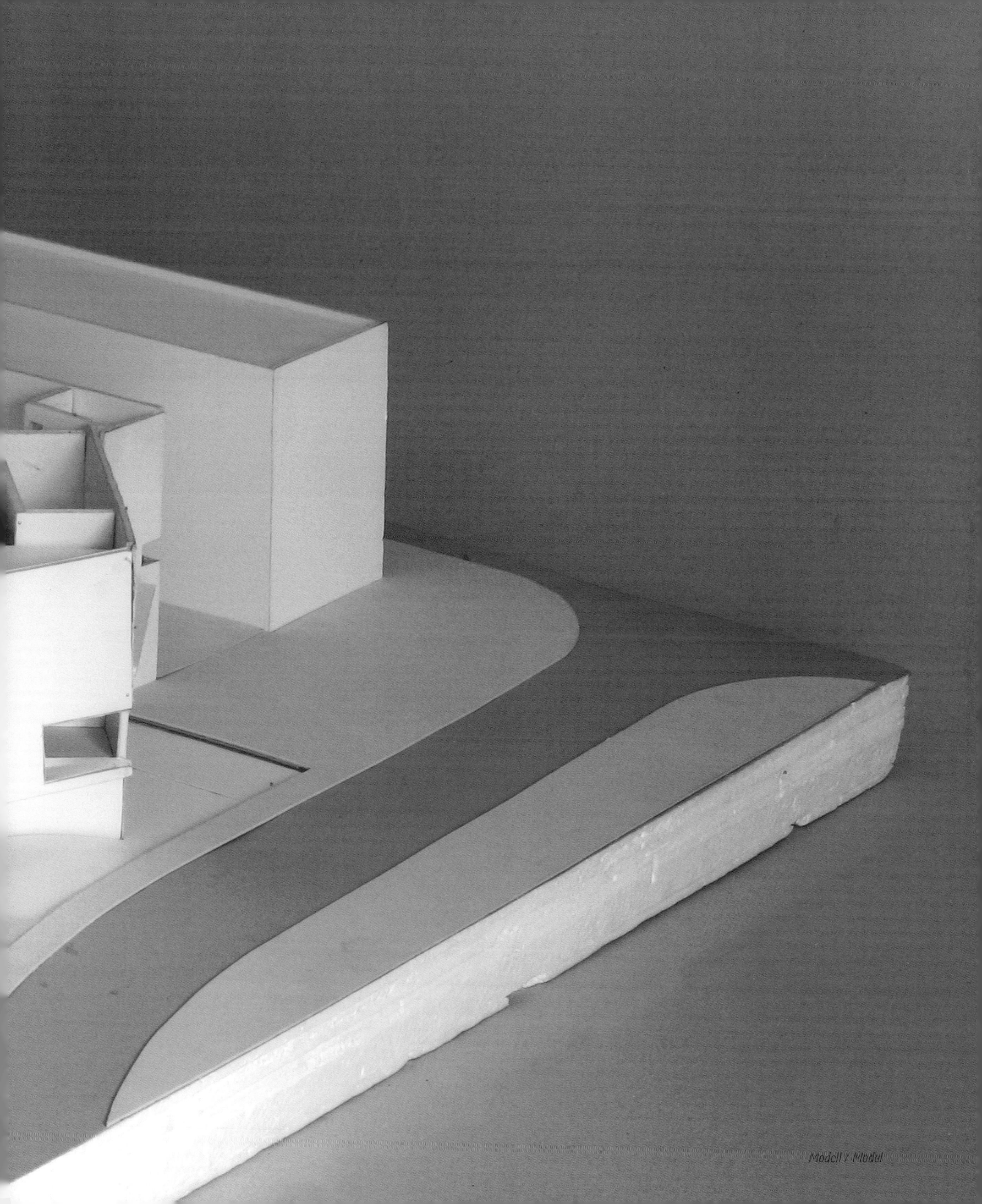

Ostgallerie / East gallery

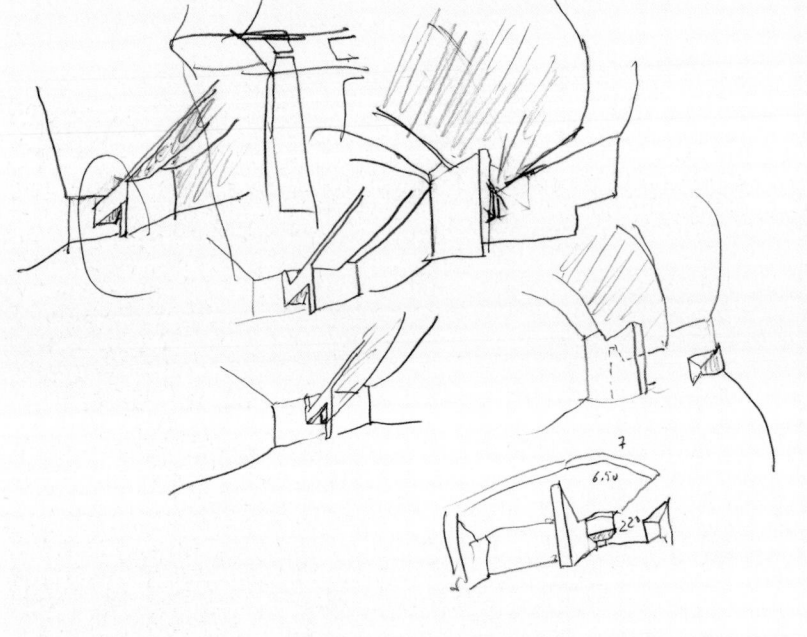

Skizzen Ausstellungsraum / Exhibition space sketches

Haupttreppe / Main staircase

104 **Museum Mimesis**

Grundriss Erdgeschoss / Ground floor plan

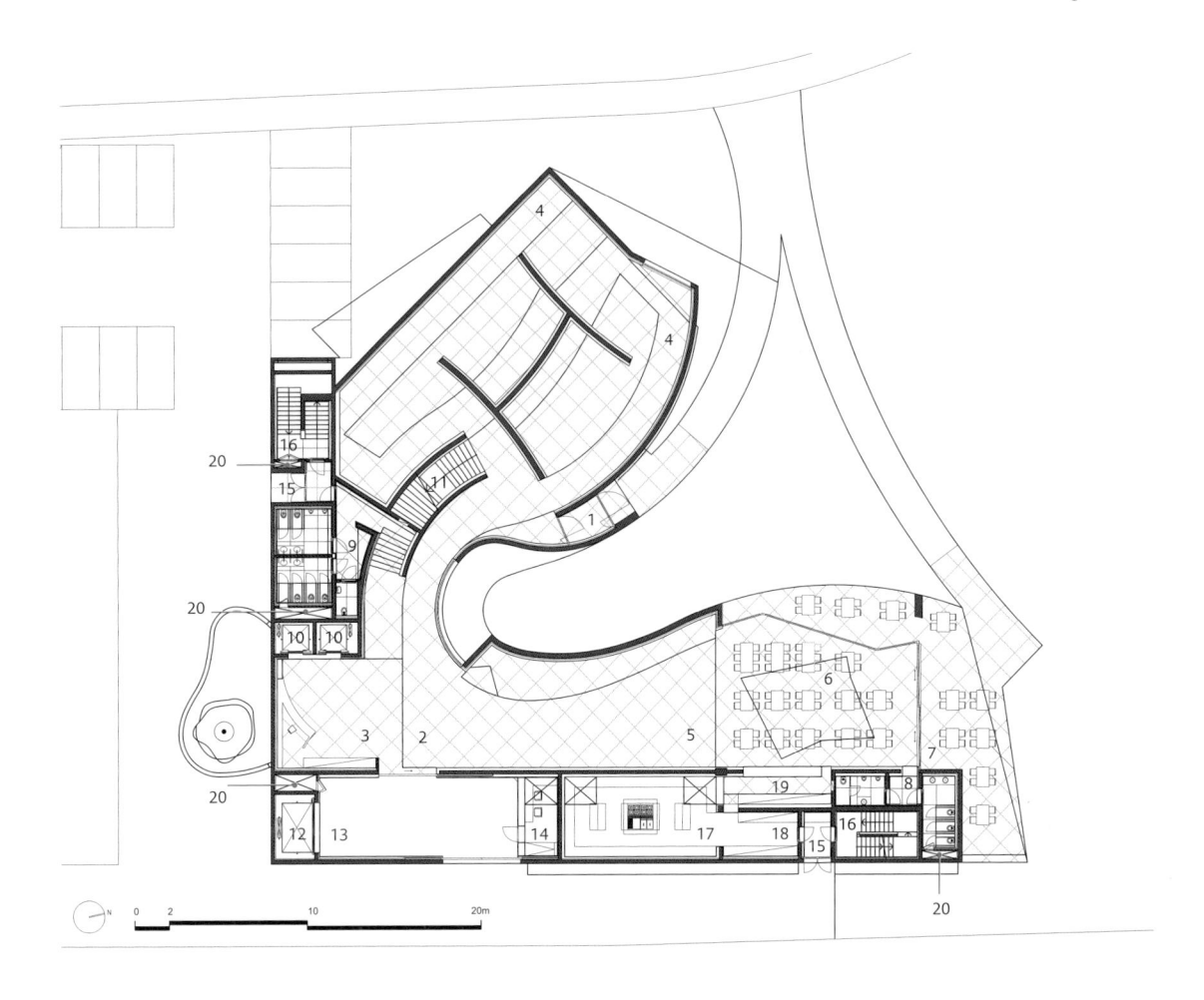

1	Öffentlicher Eingang	1	Public Entrance
2	Hauptfoyer	2	Main Foyer
3	Empfang / Garderoben	3	Reception / Cloakrooms
4	Wechselausstellungen	4	Temporary Exhibitions
5	Wechselausstellungen	5	Temporary Exhibitions
6	Café / Restaurant	6	Café / Restaurant
7	Terrasse	7	Terrace
8	öffentliche Toiletten	8	Public Toilets
9	öffentliche Toiletten	9	Public Toilets
10	öffentliche Aufzüge	10	Public Lifts
11	Treppe Zum Zwischengeschoss	11	Stair To Mezzanine
12	Lastenaufzug	12	Freight Lift
13	Laderampe	13	Loading Bay
14	Sicherheitsraum	14	Security Room
15	Service Eingang	15	Service Entrance
16	Service Treppe	16	Service Staircase
17	Küche	17	Kitchen
18	Speisekammer	18	Pantry
19	Service	19	Service
20	Versorgungsschacht	20	Vertical Ducts

Ausstellungsraum / Exhibition space

Museum Mimesis

Gesamtmodell / Complete model

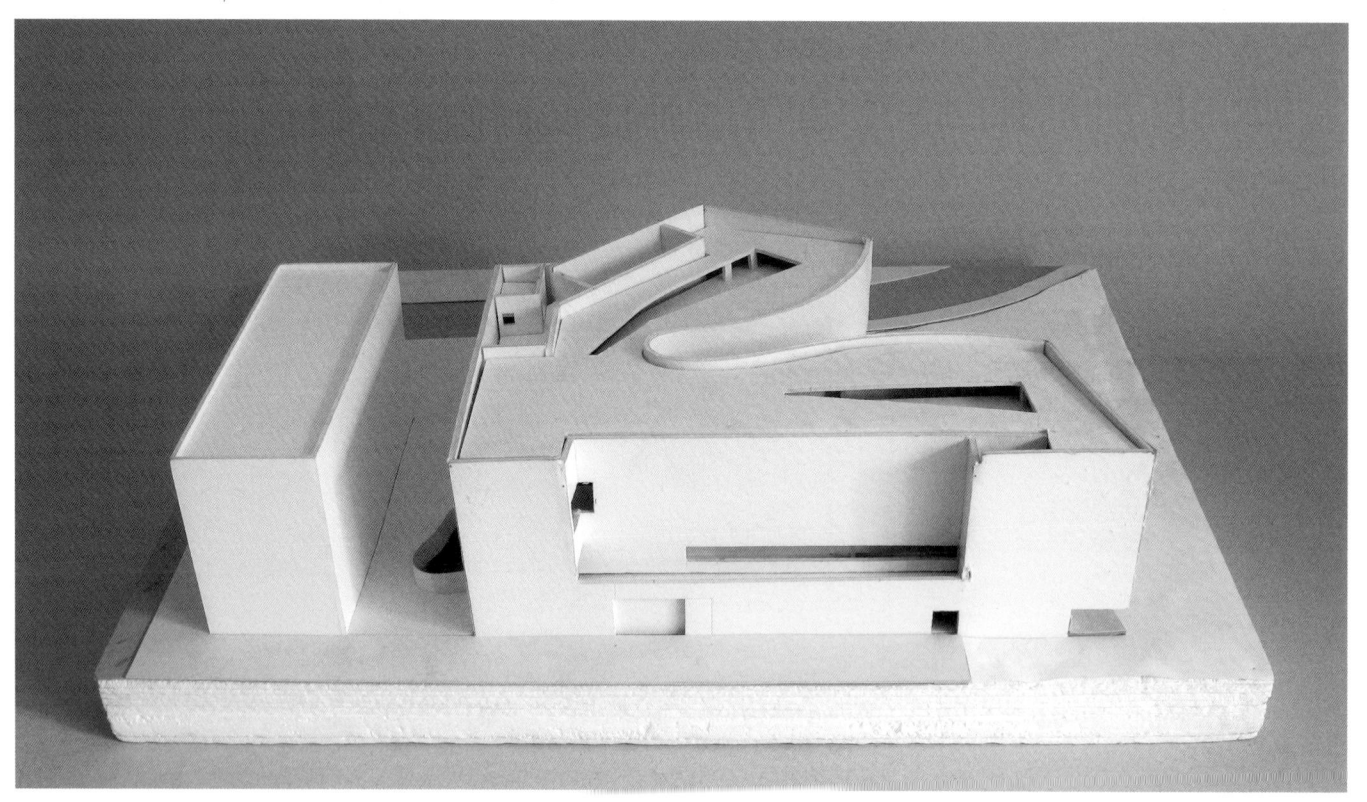

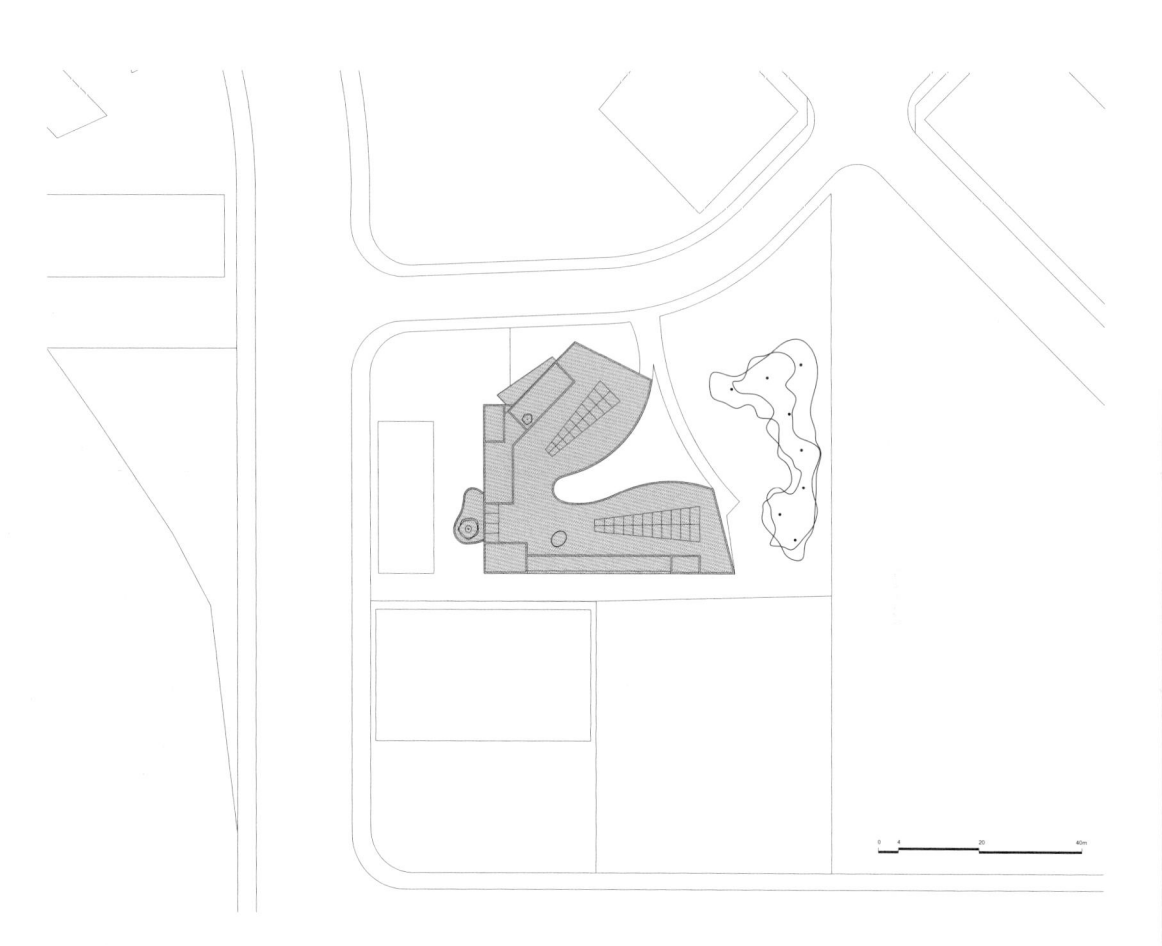

Lageplan / Site plan

Innenhof / Exterior courtyard

106 Museum Mimesis

Fenster Cafeteria / Window to Cafe

Wettbewerb Puerta Nueva
Alhambra, Spanien (2011–) 1. Preis

Competition Puerta Nueva
Alhambra, Spain (2011–) 1st Prize

Die architektonische Struktur der Alhambra ist das Ergebnis der Überlagerung einer regelmäßigen Geometrie auf eine Topographie. Zu Beginn stand die orthogonale und regelmäßige Struktur des arabischen Palastes beim Entwurf Pate, komponiert aus einer Sequenz von geschlossenen untereinander vernetzten Höfen; später kam dann jene des Palasts von Carlos V hinzu, einer phantastische Konstruktion um einen runden Innenhof, errichtet auf der urbanen, islamischen Grundstruktur. Das eine wie das andere Ordnungssystem repräsentiert die Besetzung eines Geländes durch das Einfügen einer Geometrie von Körper und Raum. Beim Eingriff in die unmittelbare Nachbarschaft der Alhambra war Álvaro Siza zunächst vom Bestand und seiner zeitgeschichtlichen Entwicklung fasziniert, hegte dann aber den Wunsch, sich davon zu befreien, ähnlich wie Machucas Projekt für den Palast von Carlos V. Im Kontext eines radikalen Wandels handelte es sich aber damals, anders als heute, um einen Eingriff, der eine fundamentale Veränderung der Machtverhältnisse symbolisierte.

Aktuell wird beabsichtigt, alle Zugänge und Diensträume, die für eine sehr große Anzahl von Besuchern geöffnet sind, für die die Alhambra ein Mythos und ein Wunschziel ist, zu ordnen und zu verbessern. Der neue Zugang zur Alhambra muss sich in ein delikates Gleichgewicht zwischen Natur und Architektur einfügen. Der Palast von Carlos V ist ein deutlicher und radikaler Ausdruck für die neuen Machtverhältnisse. Die Meisterschaft des Architekten hat dazu geführt, dass im Verhältnis zu dem, was die Alhambra einmal war, nämlich ein extrem merkwürdiger Baukörper mit autonomem Ausdruck und andersartigem Maßstab, die Qualität des Ensembles durch den neuen Zugang erhöht wurde. Er verändert, zerstört aber nicht, sondern stellt den Charakter eines architektonischen Komplexes wieder her. Der Eingriff beabsichtigt, eine Empfangssituation für die Besucher zu schaffen, eine Erweiterung, die technisch auf der Höhe der Zeit ist. Der Vorschlag antwortet auf verschiedene Maßstäbe und Interessen: zum einen auf die Beziehungen zur bestehenden Alhambra und zur umgebenden Landschaft und zum anderen auf die Beziehungen zur näheren Umgebung und ihren Besonderheiten. Es wird eine Architektur vorgeschlagen, die sich in die Landschaft integriert und die »Plaza de la Alhambra« neu organisiert. Der neue Empfangsbereich wird Teil des »Zugangsparks«, eines begrünten Weges mit Bäumen und Wasserelementen. Der Entwurf des neuen Atriums verbindet Architektur und Landschaft und bezieht Blickachsen und Ausblicke auf die Alhambra mit ein. Das neue Atrium versteht sich als Tor zum Monument, als ein Aussichtspark über die Alhambra. Die Organisation der Gebäude sieht eine Nutzungsverteilung und keine Konzentration auf ein einzelnes Bauwerk vor. Ein Hauptziel ist es, die Zufahrten für Bus, Auto, Fußgänger neu zu organisieren und die Ströme mit der vorhandenen Topographie zu koordinieren. Mittels Räumen für Information, Kultur und Freizeit soll die Besuchersituation durch den Eingriff verbessert werden. Der Entwurf integriert die Parkplatzsituation in ein landschaftliches Bild von Bäumen und Wasserelementen, das Parkplatzangebot wird unterirdisch erweitert. Der Vorschlag berücksichtigt den vorhandenen Baumbestand und verdichtet ihn. Für den Bau des Atriums werden Materialien und konstruktive Lösungen aus dem Bestand der Alhambra vorgeschlagen. Die Entwicklung in die Zukunft, mit neuen Wegen für Transport, einem Kulturbereich und andere Themen sind in dem Vorschlag bereits mitberücksichtigt.

Ansicht von Westen / West elevation

The architectural structure of the Alhambra is the result of a superimposition of a regular geometry on top of a topography. At the beginning, the orthogonal and regular structure of the Arabic palace was the force behind the design, composed on the basis of a sequence of closed and interconnected courtyards; later the structure of the palace of Carlos V was added, a fantastic construction around a circular court, built upon the underlying urban, Islamic foundations. Both ordering systems represent the occupation of a territory via the introduction of a geometric system of solids and voids.   Intervening in the immediate surroundings of the Alhambra, Álvaro Siza was at first fascinated by the historic development, then, however, driven by the wish to be liberated from this, analogous to Machuca's project for the palace of Carlos V. In the context of a radical change, the intervention then, quite in contrast to today, symbolized a fundamental change in the relationship of power.   Today, the intention is to order and improve all entrances and service spaces, which are open to a very large number of visitors, for whom the Alhambra is a myth and a dream destination. The new entrance to the Alhambra has to submit itself to the delicate balance between nature and architecture.   The palace of Carlos V is a clear and radical expression of a new relationship of power. The architect's mastery led to a situation which, compared to the status that the Alhambra once had, namely to a be an extremely strange building configuration with an unusual sense of scale, increases the quality of the overall complex by means of the addition of the new entrance element. The latter changes the situation, however, it does not destroy, on the contrary, it refreshes the character of the architectural complex.

The intervention intends to create a welcoming situation for visitors, an extension which, in technical terms, is of the highest standards of our time.   The project deals with different orders of scale and spheres of interests: for one, it deals with the relationship of the intervention with the existing Alhambra and with the surrounding landscape, and for another, with the relationship to the immediate surroundings and their specificities.   The intervention proposes an architecture which integrates itself into the landscape and which reorganizes the "Plaza de la Alhambra".

The new reception area becomes part of the "approach park", a landscaped path with trees and water elements.   The design of the new atrium brings together architecture and landscape, and integrates sightlines and views of the Alhambra.   The new atrium is to be understood as a gate to the monument, as a belvedere park from which the Alhambra is to be viewed.   The organization of the buildings foresees a distribution of uses and not a concentration of these within a single building.   The main aim is to reorganize the access routes for buses, cars and pedestrians, and to coordinate their flows within the existing topography.   The situation of the visitors is to be improved by means of providing spaces for information, culture and leisure.   The design integrates the car parking within a landscape composition of trees and water elements, while the range of car parking options is extended below ground.   The proposal respects the existing trees and increases their presence. Materials and constructional details are taken from the existing buildings of the Alhambra for the construction of the atrium.

Future developmental phases, including new routes for transport, a cultural area and other themes, have been included in this proposal.

Zugang / Access

Besucherzugang / Visitors access

Skizze Innenraum / Interior sketch ▸

110   **Wettbewerb Alhambra**

Competition Alhambra 111

Lageplan / Site plan

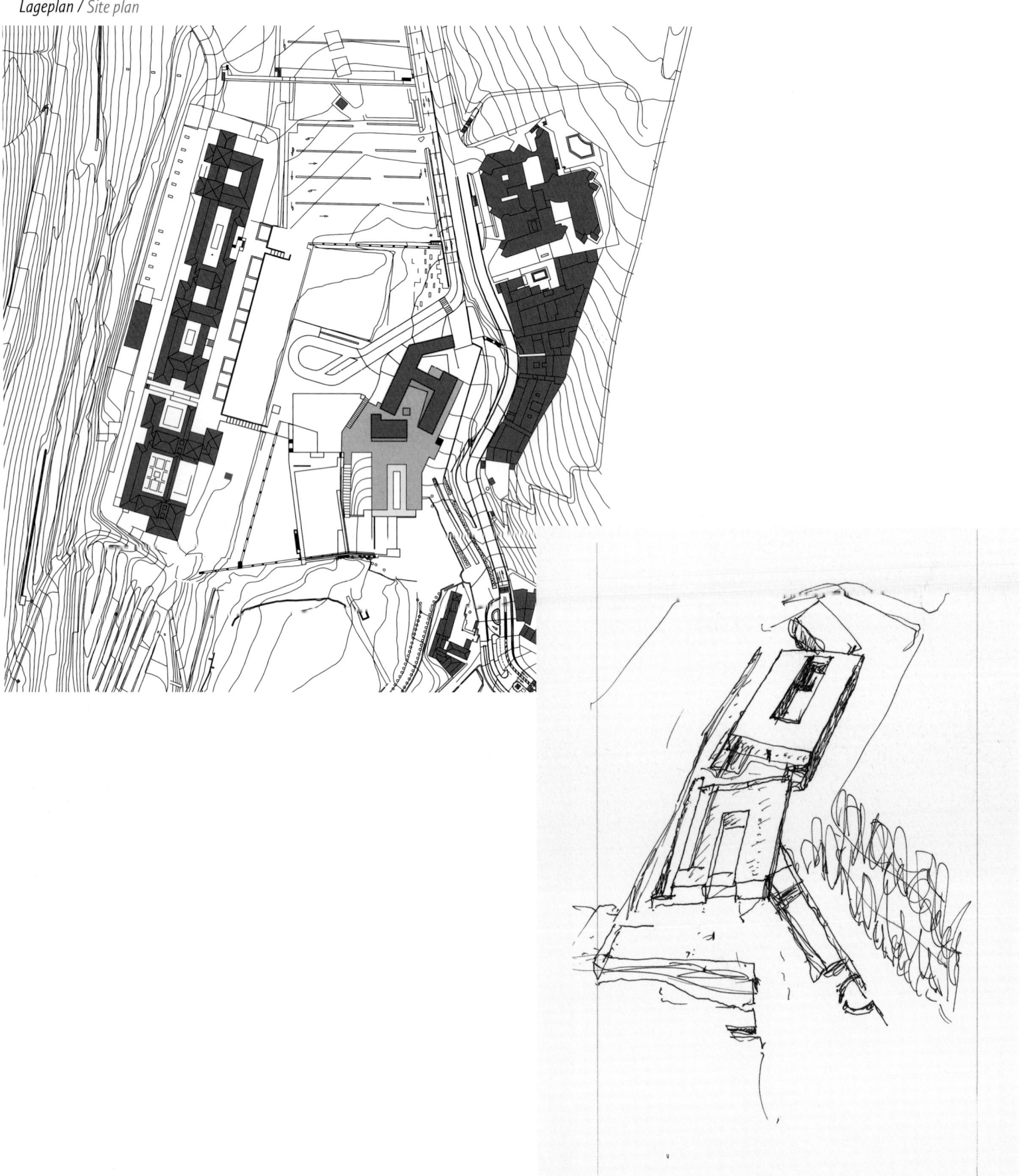

Volumenstudie / Study of volumes

112 **Wettbewerb Alhambra**

Geländemodell / Site model

Competition Alhambra

Grundriss Hauptebene / Floor plan main level

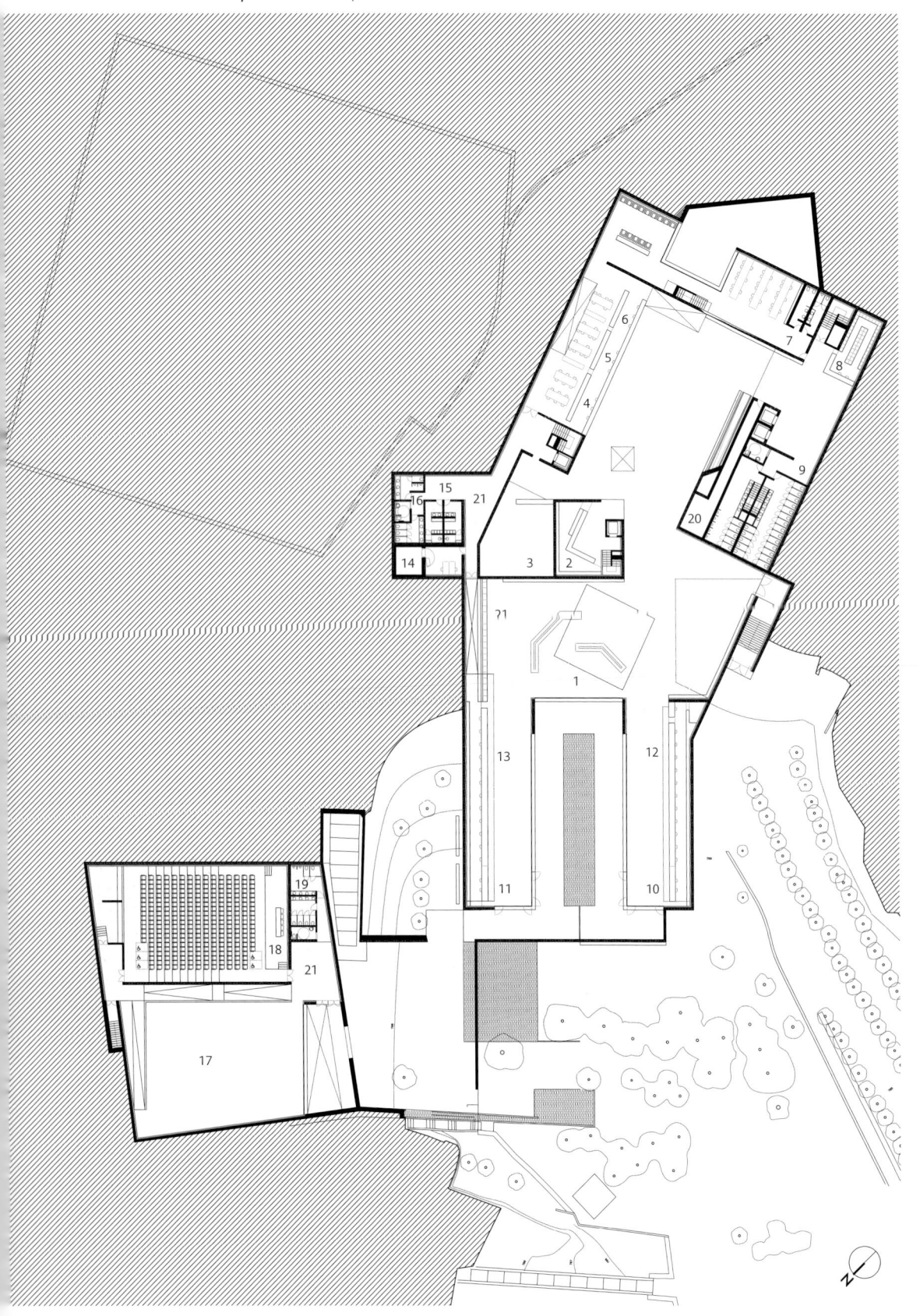

1	*Empfangshalle*	*(1454 m²)*
2	*Cafeteria*	*(66 m²)*
3	*Tourist Information*	*(90 m²)*
4	*Reiseleitung*	*(70 m²)*
5	*Kulturelle Aktivitäten*	*(52 m²)*
6	*Auskunft*	*(242 m²)*
7	*WC (Personal)*	*(16 m²)*
8	*Kontrolle / Sicherheitsraum*	*(33 m²)*
9	*WC*	*(100 m²)*
10	*Audioguide*	*(14 m²)*
11	*Audioguide*	*(14 m²)*
12	*Schließfächer*	*(160 m²)*
13	*Schließfächer + Fahrkartenautomaten*	*(97 m²)*
14	*Tresor*	*(28 m²)*
15	*Garderobe*	*(22 m²)*
16	*WC (Personal)*	*(25 m²)*
17	*Alhambra Präsentationsraum*	*(350 m²)*
18	*Konferenzraum*	*(342 m²)*
19	*WC*	*(39 m²)*
20	*Brandschutzraum*	*(15 m²)*
21	*Kommunikationsbereich Ebene 0*	*(231 m²)*

1	*Reception Hall*	*(1454 m²)*
2	*Cafeteria*	*(66 m²)*
3	*Tourist Information*	*(90 m²)*
4	*Tour Guides*	*(70 m²)*
5	*Cultural Activities Desk*	*(52 m²)*
6	*Information Desk*	*(242 m²)*
7	*WC (Staff)*	*(16 m²)*
8	*Control / Security Room*	*(33 m²)*
9	*WC (Public)*	*(100 m²)*
10	*Audio Guide Desk*	*(14 m²)*
11	*Ausio Guide Desk*	*(14 m²)*
12	*Lockers*	*(160 m²)*
13	*Lockers + Ticket Machines*	*(97 m²)*
14	*Safe Deposit*	*(28 m²)*
15	*Cloakroom*	*(22 m²)*
16	*WC (Staff)*	*(25 m²)*
17	*Alhambra Presentation Room*	*(350 m²)*
18	*Conference Room*	*(342 m²)*
19	*WC (Public)*	*(39 m²)*
20	*Fire Safety Equipment*	*(15 m²)*
21	*Communication Area Level 0*	*(231 m²)*

Blick von Süden / South view

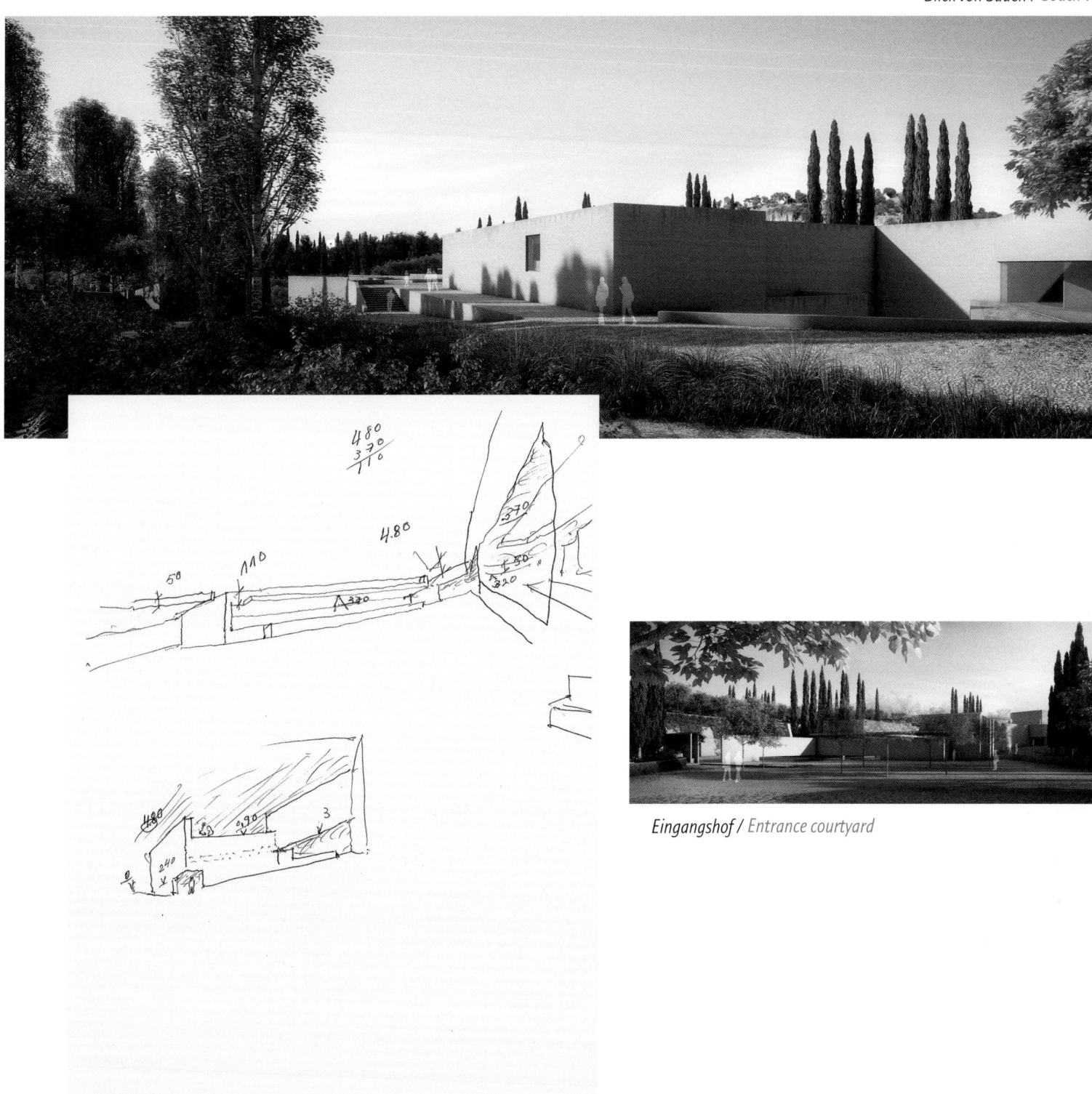

Eingangshof / Entrance courtyard

Skizzen Foyer / Foyer sketches

Competition Alhambra

Biographien

Biographies

Álvaro Siza

Álvaro Joaquim Melo Siza wurde 1933 in Matosinhos (nahe Porto) geboren. Von 1949 bis 1955 studierte er Architektur an der Universität von Porto. Er lebt und arbeitet in Porto.

Von 1955 bis 1958 war er Mitarbeiter im Büro von Arch. Fernando Távora. Er unterrichtete von 1966 bis 1969 an der School of Architecture (ESBAP) und wurde 1976 Professor für »Construction«. Er war Gastprofessor an der Ecole Polytechnique Lausanne, der University of Pennsylvania, der Los Andes University of Bogotá und der Graduate School of Design der Harvard University.

Er ist Doktor »Honoris Causa« an einer Vielzahl von Universitäten. Seine Arbeiten wurden unter anderem ausgestellt auf der Biennale von Venedig (1978, 2002, 2004); im Centre Georges Pompidou, Paris (1982); an der Internationalen Bau Ausstellung, Berlin (1984 und 1987); der Biennale von São Paolo, Brasilien (1993); im Belém Cultural Centre, Lissabon; im Museum of Architecture, Prag; auf der Triennale Mailand(2004); im Serralves Museum, Porto (2005).

Er gewann unter anderem folgende Preise: Gold Medaille der Alvar Aalto Foundation, European Award of Architecture der Europäischen Union / Mies van der Rohe Foundation, Barcelona; Pritzker Prize; National Prize of Architecture der Portugiesischen Architektenkammer 1993; Praemium Imperiale von der Japan Art Association, Tokyo; Gran-Cruz da Ordem do Infante D. Henrique der portugiesischen Republik 1999; den Goldenen Löwen der Venedig Biennale 2001; Order of Merit des brasilianischen Kultusministeriums 2007. 2009, die Royal Gold Medal 2009 der RIBA.

Er ist Mitglied der American Academy of Arts and Science, »Honorary Fellow« des Royal Institute of British Architects, AIA / American Institute of Architects, Académie d'Architecture de France und European Academy of Sciences and Arts, Royal Swedish Academy of Fine Arts.

Álvaro Joaquim Melo Siza Vieira was born in Matosinhos (near Porto), in 1933.

From 1949 to 1955, he studied at the School of Architecture, University of Porto. He lives and works in Porto.

From 1955 to 1958 he was a collaborator of Arch. Fernando Távora. He taught at the School of Architecture (ESBAP) from 1966 to 1969 and was appointed Professor of "Construction" in 1976. He has been a Visiting Professor at the Ecole Polytechnique of Lausanne, the University of Pennsylvania, Los Andes University of Bogotá and the Graduate School of Design of Harvard University.

Doctor "Honoris Causa" from a large number of universities. His work has been exhibited at the Biennales of Venice (1978, 2002, 2004); Centre Georges Pompidou, Paris (1982); International Building Exhibition, Berlin (1984 and 1987); Biennale of São Paolo, Brazil (1993); Belém Cultural Centre, Lisbon; Museum of Architecture, Prague; Triennial of Milan (2004); Serralves Museum, Porto (2005).

Prizes amongst others: Gold Medal of the Alvar Aalto Foundation, European Award of Architecture by the European Union / Mies van der Rohe Foundation, Barcelona; Pritzker Prize; National Prize of Architecture of the Portuguese Architects Association in 1993; Praemium Imperiale by the Japan Art Association, Tokyo; Gran-Cruz da Ordem do Infante D. Henrique from the Portuguese Republic in 1999; Golden Lion of the Venice Biennale 2001; Order of Merit from the Cultural Ministry of Brazil in 2007. In 2009, Royal Gold Medal 2009 by the RIBA

He is a member of the American Academy of Arts and Science, "Honorary Fellow" of the Royal Institute of British Architects, AIA/ American Institute of Architects, Académie d'Architecture de France and European Academy of Sciences and Arts, Royal Swedish Academy of Fine Arts.

Biographien
Biographies

Rudolf Finsterwalder

Rudolf Finsterwalder ist Architekt, wurde 1966 in Rosenheim geboren und lebt und arbeitet in Stephanskirchen und in Berlin. Mitarbeit in Architekturbüros in Berlin, Porto, Rom und Salzburg. Seit 2000 eigenes Architekturbüro mit Maria José Finsterwalder; verschiedene Bauten in Europa mit Schwerpunkt auf der Auseinandersetzung mit Formen und Strukturen der Natur.

Herausgeber des Buchs *form follows nature*, mit Beiträgen von u.a. Frei Otto, Carsten Nicolai.

Zu den Auszeichnungen und Preisen zählen der Rom-Preis (2007), mit Álvaro Siza der Sonderpreis brick-award (2009). Ausstellungen u.a. 9. Architekturbiennale Venedig (2004), AIA New York (2005), Insel Hombroich (2005), Museum Ludwig (2008), 11. Architekturbiennale Venedig (2010), Martin-Gropius-Bau Berlin (2011).

Rudolf Finsterwalder is an architect, was born in 1966 in Rosenheim. He lives and works in Stephanskirchen and in Berlin. Collaborator in architectural offices in Berlin, Porto, Rome and Salzburg. Since 2000 he heads his own office with Maria José Finsterwalder; has realized a variety of buildings in Europe with an emphasis on the exchange between forms and structures found in nature.

Editor of the book *form follows nature* with contributions from Frei Otto, Carsten Nicolai and others.

Awards and prizes include the Rome Prize (2007), with Álvaro Siza a special brick-award (2009). Exhibitions include 9th Venice Architecture Biennale (2004), AIA New York (2005), Museum Island Hombroich (2005), Museum Ludwig (2008), 11th Venice Architecture Biennale (2010), Martin-Gropius-Building Berlin (2011).

Wilfried Wang

Gründer mit Barbara Hoidn des Architekturbüros *Hoidn Wang Partner* in Berlin; O'Neil Ford Centennial Professor in Architecture an der University of Texas at Austin. Geboren in Hamburg; Studium der Architektur in London; Gründungsherausgeber der Zeitschrift *9H Magazine*, Ko-Direktor der *9H Gallery* in London; Direktor des Deutschen Architektur-Museums von 1995 bis 2000.

Autor und Herausgeber verschiedener Mono- und Topographien zur Architektur des 20. Jahrhunderts. Mitherausgeber der O'Neil Ford Mono- und Duographie Reihe. Vorstandsvorsitzender der Erich-Schelling Architekturstiftung; Mitglied des Gestaltungsbeirats des Flughafens München; a.o. Mitglied des BDA; Auslandsmitglied der Königlichen Akademie der Bildenden Künste in Stockholm; Mitglied der Akademie der Künste Berlin; Dr. h.c. des Königlichen Instituts für Technologie, Stockholm.

Founder with Barbara Hoidn of *Hoidn Wang Partner* in Berlin; O'Neil Ford Centennial Professor in Architecture at the University of Texas at Austin. Born in Hamburg, studied architecture in London, founding editor of *9H Magazine*; co-director of the *9H Gallery* London; from 1995 to 2000 director of the German Architecture Museum.

Author and editor of various mono- and topographic publications on the architecture of the 20th century. Co-editor of O'Neil Ford Mono- and Duograph series. Chairman of the Board of the Schelling Architecture Foundation; member of the design review board of Munich Airport; associated member of the BDA; foreign member of the Royal Swedish Academy of Arts; member of the Academy of the Arts Berlin; Dr. h.c. from the Royal Institute of Technology, Stockholm.

Bildnachweis | Photographic Acknowledgements

Bau | *Building*
    Tomas Riehle: 24–31
    Fernando Guerra: 37–63
    Juan Rodriguez: 72–77

Modell | *Model*
    Tomas Riehle: 25
    Rudolf Finsterwalder: 35
    Office Siza: 27 | 38, 39 | 43, 48–51 | 58, 61 | 82–85
        92, 93, 95, 96 | 102, 103 | 106
    Jorge Coelho: 78

Impressum

Arch. Rudolf Finsterwalder   www.finsterwalderarchitekten.com
Prof. Wilfried Wang   www.hoidnwang.de

Das Werk ist urheberrechtlich geschützt. Die dadurch begründeten Rechte, insbesondere die der Übersetzung, des Nachdruckes, der Entnahme von Abbildungen, der Funksendung, der Wiedergabe auf photomechanischem oder ähnlichem Wege und der Speicherung in Datenverarbeitungsanlagen, bleiben, auch bei nur auszugsweiser Verwertung, vorbehalten.

This work is subject to copyright. All rights are reserved, whether the whole or part of the material is concerned, specifically those of translation, reprinting, re-use of illustrations, broadcasting, reproduction by photocopying machines or similar means, and storage in data banks.

© 2011 Springer-Verlag / Wien
Printed in Austria
SpringerWienNewYork is a part of Springer Science + Business Media
springer.at

Verlag und Herausgeber bitten um Verständnis dafür, dass in Einzelfällen ihre Bemühungen um die Abklärung der Urheberrechte und Textzitate ohne Erfolg geblieben sind.

The publisher and editor kindly wish to inform you that in some cases, despite efforts to do so, the obtaining of copyright permissions and usage of excerpts of text is not always successful.

Die Wiedergabe von Gebrauchsnamen, Handelsnamen, Warenbezeichnungen usw. in diesem Buch berechtigt auch ohne besondere Kennzeichnung nicht zu der Annahme, dass solche Namen im Sinne der Warenzeichen- und Markenschutz-Gesetzgebung als frei zu betrachten wären und daher von jedermann benutzt werden dürfen.

Product liability: The publisher can give no guarantee for the information contained in this book. The use of registered names, trademarks, etc. in this publication does not imply, even in the absence of a specific statement, that such names are exempt from the relevant protective laws and regulations and are therefore free for general use.

Layout & Coverdesign:
Anne Schmidt (Calysto), Leipzig, Germany

Übersetzung | Translation *from German into English, English into German*: Wilfried Wang, Rudolf Finsterwalder

Mitarbeit | Collaboration: Maria Chiara Porcu, Jonathan Buckley

Lektorat | Proof reading: Michael Walch, Wien | Vienna, Austria

Bildbearbeitung | Image processing:
Manfred Kostal (Pixelstrom), Wien | Vienna, Austria

Druck | Printing: Holzhausen Druck GmbH, Wien | Vienna, Austria

Gedruckt auf säurefreiem, chlorfrei gebleichtem Papier – TCF
Printed on acid-free and chlorine-free bleached paper
SPIN: 80063176

Mit 150 Abbildungen
With 150 illustrations

Bibliografische Informationen der Deutschen Nationalbibliothek
Die Deutsche Nationalbibliothek verzeichnet diese Publikation in der Deutschen Nationalbibliografie; detaillierte bibliografische Daten sind im Internet über <http://dnb.ddb.de> abrufbar.

ISBN 978-3-7091-0853-6 SpringerWienNewYork

Unser Dank gilt den Sponsoren
We thank our sponsors:

vitra.

HEIDELBERGER BETON
HEIDELBERGCEMENT Group

FSB

Wienerberger
Ziegel. Für uns Menschen gemacht.

Förderverein
der Insel Hombroich

und

Stiftung
Insel Hombroich